CHRISTMAS
WITH ELVIS

By Jim Curtin
with Renata Ginter

Published by
Celebrity Books
a division of Hambleton-Hill Publishing, Inc.
1501 County Hospital Road
Nashville, TN 37218

For a free catalog of titles
or to order more copies of this book,
please call (800) 327-5113

ISBN: 1-58029-104-X

Library of Congress Cataloging-in-Publication Data:
Curtin, Jim.
Christmas with Elvis / by Jim Curtin with Renata Ginter.
p. cm.
Discography: p.
ISBN 1-58029-104-X
1. Presley, Elvis, 1935-1977--Miscellanea. 2. Christmas--Miscellanea. I. Ginter, Renata. II. Title.
ML420.P96C89 1999
782.42166'092--dc21
[B] 98-27720
CIP
MN

Cover design: Laughlin Studios
All photos from the collection of James J. Curtin Archives,
The Elvis Empire™

First printing, October 1999

10 9 8 7 6 5 4 3 2 1

Dedications

Dedicated to the life, career, and memory of
Colonel Thomas Parker.
He always wanted Elvis to do a Christmas special
for all the world to enjoy. Colonel, here is your wish,
a tribute that will make every Christmas special, now and forever.

Dedicated to my beloved parents,
Louise M. Curtin and James J. Curtin, Jr.

A special dedication to Lisa Marie Presley,
who through this book
can now spend every Christmas with her father, Elvis.

Another special dedication to all the Elvis fans,
because you have made it your business
to keep the memory of Elvis alive.

Last but certainly not least,
to Elvis Aron Presley
who loved this holiday more than anyone.
Elvis...this one's for you, my friend.

—Jim Curtin

Christmas Quotes by Elvis

"Before we do this song, I'd like to tell everybody that they've made this the best Christmas that I've ever had. We'd like to thank everybody for all the presents and Christmas cards and birthday cards that came in. I got exactly 282 teddy bears during the Christmas holidays. We have the walls lined with them. I'd like to tell you that we deeply appreciate it—that we're sorry we couldn't give every one of you a new Lincoln, but they wouldn't sell us that many!" (January 6, 1957, on *The Ed Sullivan Show*)

"I recall, when I was a small child, we got several of our dinner glasses from oatmeal boxes for one Christmas. They were a real gift because they didn't cost us anything. They came in rather handy at mealtime!"

"My Mama and I used to plan Christmas for days, even when we had no money at all!"

"We had a Christmas party here. I had a lot of guys from over at the post, you know. I had as many of the boys here as possible at my home... to kind of make them feel at home around Christmastime. And we had a little Christmas party and on New Year's we had another little party and it seemed nice. It was better than last year!" (1959, while in the Army in Germany)

"I'm looking forward to spending this coming Christmas in a new way. I'm looking forward to possibly seeing some people that are gonna be shocked. I just hope they're not gonna be hurt, but I know they're gonna be shocked!" (1960, referring to Priscilla's first visit to Graceland)

"Christmas is my favorite holiday. I believed in Santa Claus until I was eight years old. Some of the kids at school told me that there was no such thing. Mama explained it to me in such a way that Christmas didn't lose its magic." (1961)

"I am not the only boy to lose his mother and I am well aware that there are so many others, but I can never show the grief I feel inside. And Christmas, which meant so much to us, because Mama made it such a wonderful, big, happy occasion, brings back that grief." (1961)

"On holidays, I miss her the most. At Graceland we make the most of Christmas. So far I've had the good luck to be sure I am always home for Christmas. That has always been a rule!" (1965, speaking of his mother)

"Home means all the relatives and friends getting together and all of us talking and laughing and singing and playing and enjoying ourselves. Like Christmas, everyone was at Graceland. And the boys, they have wives and children and families, just everyone. We had a great time. We had turkeys and a huge Christmas tree of course. And lots of presents." (1965)

"Sure I go Christmas shopping! My mama and I used to plan Christmas for days and we'd work out every detail together. I enjoy it. Although the big revolving Christmas tree that Mama loved so much has been stored away in the attic at Graceland, it has to be replaced by a new one. The other one broke. It has lots of sentiment for me for I always see my mother sitting in the kitchen doorway in her chair looking at the tree and loving the lights twinkling round and round as it turns and the Christmas carols playing from the music box in it. I intend to keep it." (1965)

"My Mama could take a quarter's worth of meat and make it taste like the finest turkey in the world for the Christmases we were too poor to have anything more. She always held a little something back somehow, so we always had a fine Christmas and a good Thanksgiving." (1965)

"There is a lot of difference in Christmas today and when we were growing up in East Tupelo. Honestly, I can't say that these are any better!"

"... The Christmas carols, trees and lights just grab you. There is something about Christmas and being home that I just can't explain. Maybe it's being with the family and with friends. And of course there are the snowball fights and sleigh rides and yes, just Home!" (1966)

"Christmas is really the best season of the year!"

1960's RCA Christmas postcard. Given to all major record stores in the U.S. to give out to customers.

Contents

Elvis, 1956.

Introduction

Christmas has always meant family gatherings, gift giving, and well wishing. We may choose to celebrate it with a tree decorated with our memories and multi-colored lights and presents placed underneath. Old traditions passed on to us from generations past and new ones created with our families and friends make this the most special of all holidays. Old Saint Nicholas is still alive in our hearts as we joyfully wrap gifts in brightly colored paper, and memories of Christmases past sometimes bring tears to our eyes as we think of those who have shared our lives and hearts.

No one enjoyed this holiday time more than Elvis Aron Presley. As a child, Elvis was able to see past the poverty and, with the help of his parents, made this day something grand. Their financial difficulties were forgotten about, their troubles gone when Christmas rolled around. The Presleys spent days preparing for it, planning lists of presents, favorite foods, and ways to make it special. As a result, Elvis grew up with a strong feeling towards Christmas. He wanted it to be the best it could be for everyone. He donated to charities every year to help the sick and needy. Within his own household, he went all out, buying diamonds, jewelry, cars, furs, and homes for his family, fans, and friends. Many thought he was crazy for giving away so much, but to Elvis it meant sharing his wealth, happiness, and the spirit of Christmas.

In this book, you will read many wonderful recollections about Elvis during this joyous holiday that I have gathered throughout the years. You will also see the many rare and one-of-a-kind photos of Elvis at Christmastime taken by fans, along with priceless collectibles from 1956 to the present, from all over the world, from my personal collection and archives.

It is my hope that through this book you will spend Christmas with Elvis year after year...and that you will enjoy reminiscing with the first and only Elvis Christmas book.

Jim Curtin

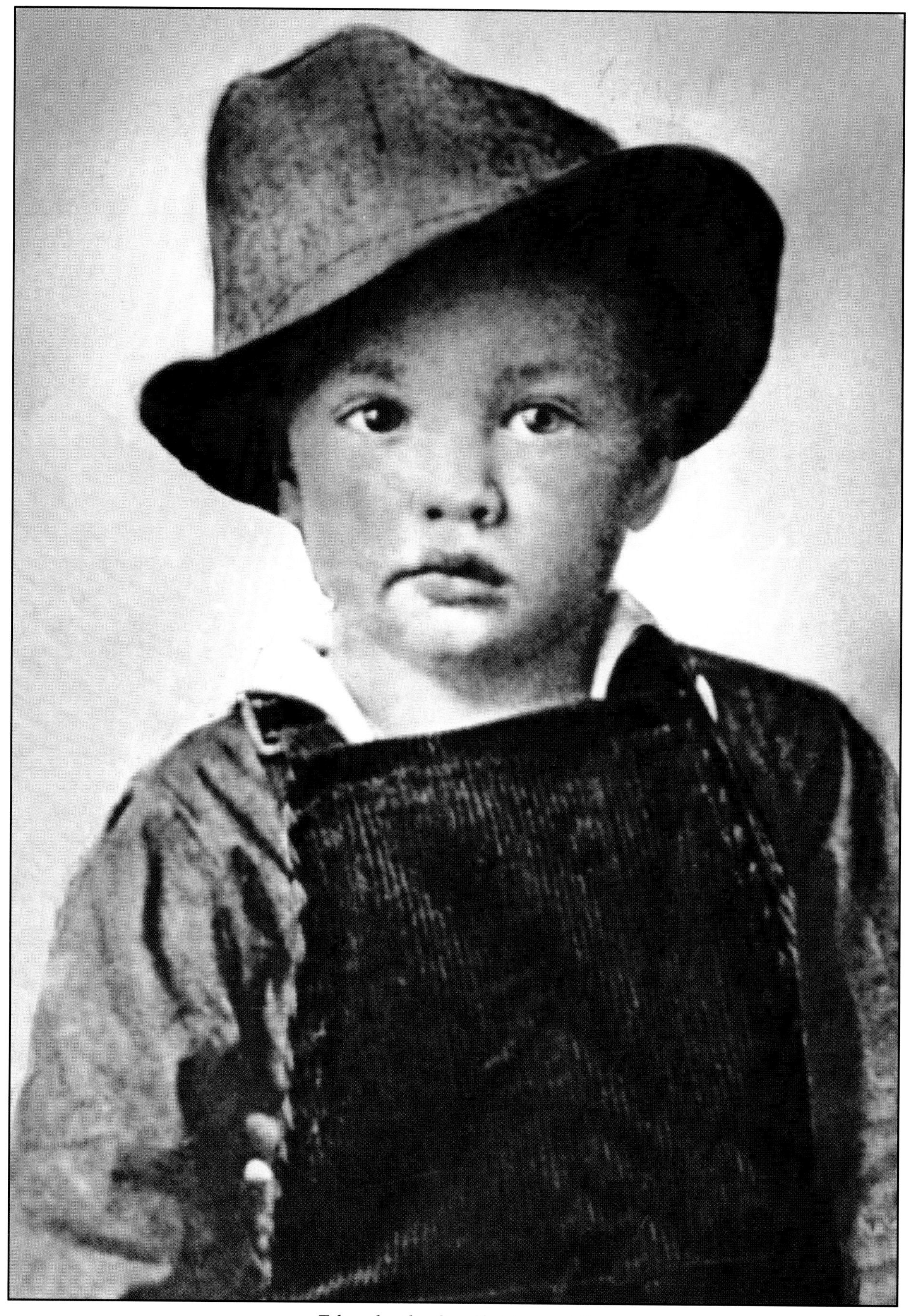

Taken shortly after Christmas 1937.

Chapter 1
Christmas in Tupelo

In the 1930's, The Good Fellows organization donated toys to the poor children of Tupelo, Mississippi. One Christmas, they made a special trip to the Presleys' shotgun shack to drop off a package for young Elvis. Gladys hid the gifts from her son until Christmas Day, at which time she presented the toys and candy to Elvis with the explanation that Santa Claus had dropped them off the night before.

In 1940, when Elvis was five years old, he received a wind-up toy train set from his parents for Christmas. He was so excited over it that he had his father, Vernon, set it up right away, and he played with it for hours, not wanting to leave it for dinner. The train set was so loved by Elvis that it was left set up all year long so that he could play with it anytime he wished to.

For Christmas in 1941, a six-year-old Elvis was given a red tricycle by his parents. Elvis was thrilled to finally own his own trike just like the other kids at school. Several weeks later, however, the tricycle disappeared not once, but twice. Both times Elvis had given the treasured trike to needy friends. At first he was lectured about giving away such an expensive gift and the trike was retrieved, but after the second incident, Vernon and Gladys realized that Elvis was being unselfish and charitable, qualities they had instilled in their son. They allowed Elvis's friend to keep the tricycle and they praised their son for having such a big heart, but they also made the point that he would not be getting another one for a long time to come.

One Christmas when Elvis was a young boy, a local charity sent the Presleys a Christmas gift basket. Vernon was unemployed at the time and the Presleys were struggling to make ends meet. Everyone in Tupelo knew about the Presleys' situation, so several of the townspeople took it upon themselves to gather a collection of food, toys, and a small amount of money, which they wrapped in a large basket. The Presleys were proud people, and even though they were embarrassed, they graciously accepted the gift. It turned out to be one of their best Christmases.

A very young Elvis found out that there was no Santa Claus from one of his cousins. When she told him that it was his mother and father who were playing the role of Santa, Elvis ran home crying. When Gladys found out what happened, she explained to her young son that there was a St. Nicholas who had lived many years ago and that he now lived on as Santa Claus in the hearts of children all over the world. His mother's explanation had Elvis jumping with glee, as it renewed his faith that there really was a Santa Claus.

Right before Christmas break in 1947, Elvis's school decided to exchange Christmas presents amongst the students. Elvis received the name of one of his best friends, Roland Tindall. Due to the Presleys financial situation, there was nothing left over to spend on a Christmas gift for Elvis's friend, so Elvis decided to give Roland his favorite blue toy truck. After scrubbing the truck to make it look like new, Elvis wrapped the gift in a brown paper bag. The next day, he took the gift to school and presented it to his friend. Elvis was heartbroken that he had to give up his only truck, but also knew it was the only way he had to give Roland a gift. It is reported that Roland still has that truck today!

The Presleys used natural decorations for their holiday Christmas trees. Vernon and his brother Vester would go hunting for a nice-sized tree, chop it down, and bring it home. Gladys and Elvis would then decorate it with berries, strung popcorn, and chains made from colored paper. To the Presley family, theirs was the best looking tree around.

When Elvis was 13 years old, he and his family were preparing to spend their first Christmas in Tennessee. Gladys wanted to make the holiday special, so she decided that they should go back to Mississippi to see their families. As Vernon had been unable to find work since their arrival in Memphis three months earlier, they had no money for the trip and were forced to hitchhike the 100-plus miles back to Tupelo. Gladys and Elvis were thrilled with the trip, as during the trek down the long, desolate highway, they discussed what they would eat and how they would sing and play with everyone. Vernon, on the other hand, complained about his feet as they walked. The soles of his shoes were completely worn out and he could not handle walking in the cold. Just as he was about to give up and force his wife and child to stop walking, a big gas truck slowed down and stopped. The driver transported them all the way to their old hometown. Once there, the Presleys hitched another ride which took them directly to their family's home on Old Saltillo Road, where they spent a festive Christmas.

Elvis holding the red wagon he got for Christmas in 1942.

Rare family Christmas card sent directly by Elvis in the 1960's.

Inside of Elvis's Christmas card from the 1960's.

Chapter 2
A Family Christmas

In 1950, a fifteen-year-old Elvis worked several odd jobs to earn some spending money for the Christmas holidays. He managed to save $15 from various jobs and bought his mother a picture of Jesus imported from Mexico. Gladys was touched by her son's thoughtfulness and resourcefulness.

After graduating from high school in June of 1953, Elvis got a job as a truck driver for Crown Electric Company. He put aside a small portion of his check each week, and when Christmastime came he was able to buy a dress for his mother. Gladys cried as she held the garment close to her chest. Excited, Elvis asked her to try the dress on. Several minutes later, he gave a loud whistle of approval when his mother came out and modeled the dress. Gladys thanked her son for spending his hard-earned money on such a beautiful Christmas gift for her.

In 1954, the Presleys spent their Christmas in a house located at 2414 Lamar Avenue in Memphis. It was the first time since moving to Memphis that they did not spend the holiday in an apartment or housing unit. They counted the house as their Christmas gift from God. It was to be their last poor Christmas.

Elvis purchased his first public Christmas cards from Bill Morris. These cards, sent out to his family and fans, were the first he sent after he became famous. Morris worked for a printing company in Memphis in the late 1950's. In the late 1960's and early 1970's, Bill Morris served as the Mayor of Memphis and county sheriff.

Colonel Parker hired a professional photographer to take photos of Elvis and his family at Christmas in 1956. He then had the photos sent out on the wire services so that they would be printed in as many publications as possible. The photos allowed the public to catch the first candid glimpse of their idol at home during the holidays. This was the only time that professional photos were taken of Elvis and his family at the Audubon house during the holidays.

For Christmas in 1956, Elvis gave his mother several gowns and a 60-piece set of fine china, the first she had ever owned. She considered the china a status symbol, as she had grown up believing that only the "well-to-do" owned fine china. For his father, Elvis purchased a diamond ring and two suits. Vernon, who had always been a fastidious dresser, put on the ring and one of the suits and, preening for Gladys, asking if she liked the new 'Diamond Vernon.'

Elvis tried to buy his mother a mink coat for Christmas in 1956. Gladys told her son that she could not see herself wearing a dead animal around her neck, parading around as the rich folk did. She forbade Elvis to buy her anything of the sort and told him not to spend his money on frivolous items. The day after Christmas, Elvis went out and bought his mother the mink coat despite her pleadings. Gladys was speechless when she opened the huge box and saw the fur. She put the coat on and modeled for her two men, asking them what they thought of their "movie star."

For their first Christmas at Graceland in 1957, Elvis bought his mother a revolving musical Christmas tree made of white nylon. Gladys had fallen in love with the tree the minute she'd seen it displayed in the store, and Elvis, seeing the look of delight on his mother's face, bought it for her. They set it up in the dining room. Gladys loved the way it revolved and played Christmas carols. She decorated the tree with red glass balls and tinsel and delighted in surrounding it with the hundreds of presents that poured in from Elvis's fans. Elvis received so many packages that most of them had to be stored in the attic until it was time to open them.

From 1957 on, Graceland was always beautifully decorated for the holidays with red velvet curtains hanging in every room and green holly wrapped around the banisters and doorways. Elvis ordered red poinsettias to decorate all the tables and the mantle in the living room, along with a few dozen red roses for his mother. Graceland was surely one of the best dressed houses in all of Tennessee.

After Elvis bought Graceland, Gladys made a vow to do the cooking for all the festive Christmas dinners at their new home. That first Christmas the Presleys lived at the mansion, she baked a turkey with all the trimmings and would not allow anyone to help her. She also forbade anyone from being in the kitchen until dinner was ready. After his mother's death the following year, Elvis would never allow anyone to cook a Christmas dinner at Graceland, so he had the holiday dinners catered.

For Christmas in 1957, Elvis bought his mother a 100-piece silverware set, a carving set with pearl handles, and a soft pink lounging gown. This last gift turned out to be too small, and Elvis scolded himself for not knowing his mother's correct size. What he did not know, however, was that Gladys had gained weight as a result of her illness. In order to make her son feel better, Gladys said, "Never mind, son. It's nice to know you think I'm that slim." Gladys continued to hide her illness from her son and her husband. 1957 marked the first and last Christmas she spent at Graceland; she died the following year.

In 1957, Gladys and Vernon gave their son a gold and diamond watch on Christmas Day. Later that day at the Rainbow Skate Rink, Elvis was knocked down and his watch was smashed on the hard wooden floor. All the way back to Graceland, Elvis shook his head and scolded his men for knocking him down and making him break his new watch. Gladys was hurt that Elvis had broken the only expensive thing they had ever given him, but she told her son not to worry about materialistic things. This watch was the last Christmas gift Elvis would receive from his mother.

On Christmas Day in 1957, Gladys dressed up as Santa Claus. She wore a brocade dress and a Santa hat as she distributed gifts, loving the expressions on the receivers' faces. Elvis said that his mother loved to play Santa even more than he did. After the last gift was opened, Gladys and Elvis played four of his new gospel songs. Gladys was thrilled that Elvis was recording some of the old gospel music that was such a part of their family history. Her favorite was "Peace in the Valley."

On Christmas Eve in 1957, Elvis invited Hannerl Melcher, Miss Austria 1957, and Kathy Gabriel, Miss Ohio 1957, to Graceland. He had liked the women when he met them and thought it would be a nice idea to share the holiday with them. Early Christmas morning, when Elvis and his friends woke up, Gladys prepared an authentic southern breakfast for them. After the huge meal, Elvis led the way into the living room so that everyone could open their gifts.

On Christmas Day 1957, Elvis took his house guest, Hannerl Melcher, on a motorcycle ride around Memphis. Hannerl wore Capri pants and slippers, while Elvis wore his leather motorcycle regalia. When they came back to Graceland, Hannerl was completely frozen. Gladys, seeing how wet and cold the girl was, scolded Elvis for being so foolish. She asked him why he had allowed the poor girl to wear such a skimpy outfit for a motorcycle ride in the middle of winter. Elvis, embarrassed and not able to answer, bowed his head in shame. Gladys then told Elvis to fetch a pair of wool socks while she dried Hannerl's feet. When Hannerl was warm and dry, Gladys went to the kitchen and made them all a hot cup of cocoa.

After Gladys's funeral in August of 1958, Elvis went up to her room in search of something that would bring his mother close to him. He went through her closet and ran his hands over the dresses that she wore, and then to her bureau where he stumbled across her unfinished Christmas list. Crying, he ran his finger over each word. When one lone tear hit the paper, mixing with the ink of her pen, Elvis folded the paper and gently put it inside his wallet. Elvis carried his mother's Christmas list with him for the rest of his life.

Fan photo Christmas card.

On Christmas Eve 1956, Elvis conducts his gift-opening ceremony with his parents, Vernon and Gladys, and his girlfriend, Dorothy Harmony.

Gladys, Vernon, and Dorothy Harmony watch Elvis as he prepares to open a Christmas present.
Christmas Eve 1956, at the Audubon Drive house.

Dorothy Harmony plays with Elvis as she hangs a ribbon from his ear. The white scarf Elvis wears is a gift from Dorothy. Christmas Eve 1956, at the 1034 Audubon Drive House.

Rare comic featuring Elvis and his girlfriend, Dorothy Harmony, along with her parents, who were also invited to spend Christmas with the Presleys in 1956.

Personal Christmas card sent by Elvis to family and friends, 1960's.

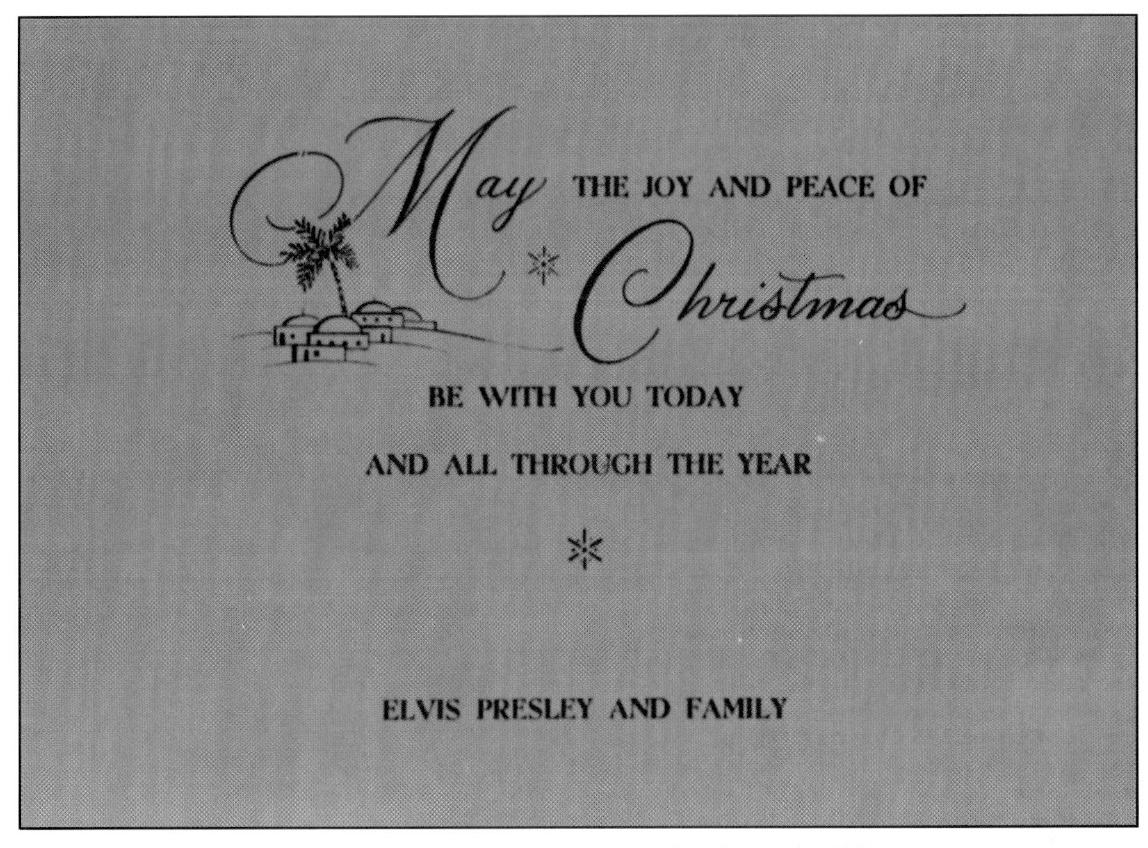

Inside of personal Christmas card sent by Elvis in the 1960's.

Collector's plate by Delphi, 1990. "Christmas at Graceland." By artist Bruce Emmett.

Chapter 3
A Rock-n-Roll Christmas

On December 23, 1949, Elvis's teacher asked him to sing and play his guitar during the school Christmas party. An excited Elvis ran home after school and practiced several songs. The next day, Elvis sang several Christmas songs and was greeted with loud applause from his fellow classmates.

The first time Elvis sang in public was at the L.C. Humes High School Christmas Minstrel on December 24, 1952. Elvis sang "Old Shep" and "Cold, Cold Icy Fingers." He surprised the entire audience, including his classmates and teachers, with his wonderful voice and singing style.

About two weeks before Christmas in 1954, Elvis was in Shreveport, Louisiana, for performances at the Louisiana Hayride. One day, he noticed a young girl selling Christmas cards on a street corner. Anxious to help her out, Elvis purchased every box she had. When the girl informed him that she could not make change for the large bill he gave her, Elvis told her to keep the change. The girl thanked him by planting a very shy but grateful kiss on his cheek.

Elvis, Scotty Moore, and Bill Black traveled to Shreveport, Louisiana, on December 23, 1954, to do a one-night show that earned each of them $100. On the drive back to Memphis, Scotty drove while Elvis slept in the back using Bill's bass as a pillow. About two hours into the drive, a state trooper pulled them over for speeding. As Elvis reminisced about this story, he remembered that he was extremely tired and that the night was very cold. Elvis feared that their hard-earned money would have to be used to pay the speeding ticket. The officer asked them for identification, and after Elvis gave him his full name, he added that he was a singer. The trooper had obviously never heard of Elvis, but he let them go with a warning anyway. After the man left, the boys got out of the car and counted their money, mostly $1 bills, in the glow from the car's headlights. None of them had ever had so much in their pockets at one time. Elvis spent every dollar on Christmas gifts for his family and friends.

Elvis performed for 150 people at the "Yuletide Jamboree" at Cook's Hoe-Down Club in Houston, Texas, on New Year's Eve in 1954. This show was special for two reasons: it was Elvis's first holiday show, and it was his last appearance in 1954. Many people liked the idea of ending the old year and starting the new year with one of Elvis's shows.

During the Christmas holidays in 1955, Elvis and the Blue Moon Boys were driving to a show when they spotted several girls selling boxes of Christmas cards on the street. Elvis asked Scotty Moore to pull the car over, and he went over to the stand. When Elvis returned, he had the girls' entire stock of cards in his arms. He told the guys that he liked them all and couldn't decide which ones he wanted.

On December 12, 1956, Elvis was mobbed by his fans when his Cadillac ran out of gas in front of a bank on Center Lane in downtown Memphis. He was trying to get some money out of the bank so that he could start his Christmas shopping, and he did not notice that the gas gauge read empty. When he got out of his car, a crowd started to gather. Soon the entire street was filled. Not knowing what to do and afraid of being attacked, Elvis started to run. Police were called in and two officers were ordered to get to Elvis and protect him. Before the men could push through the crowd, however, Elvis had managed to hail a cab that took him safely back to Graceland. Elvis sent two of his men out to retrieve his Cadillac, fill it with gas, and bring it back to Graceland. Afterwards, Elvis checked to make sure that all his cars on the estate had at least a half tank of gas. His Christmas shopping was postponed for another day.

Over 9,000 fans were on hand to witness Elvis's last performance at the Louisiana Hayride on December 16, 1956. The show was a Christmas benefit for the local YMCA. Before Elvis walked off the stage, everyone yelled their Christmas wishes to him.

A few days before Christmas in 1956, Elvis saw a Salvation Army Santa whose kettle was being ignored by passers-by. Elvis was aggravated that no one was stopping to donate to the charity at this time of year, so he walked over to the kettle, nodded his head at the Santa, and proceeded to sing Christmas carols aloud. As Elvis sang, each person who passed slipped some change into the kettle. After about an hour, Elvis saw that the kettle was filling up and he stopped singing. He extended his hand to the Santa and slipped him a $100 bill. The Santa thanked Elvis on behalf of the B'nai Brith, a Jewish charity organization.

In 1956, in an article entitled "To Hell with Elvis Presley," the *London Daily Sketch* newspaper reported that Elvis, "...refused to send a Christmas message to his English fans..." This was for some kind of popular TV show, probably *Shindig*. When Colonel Parker heard about the article, he contacted the paper and explained that Elvis would never have done such a thing and that the TV show had never contacted them about a Christmas message. Parker angrily explained that the rumors were false, that the story had hurt Elvis's feelings, and that the accusations contained in the article were outrageous. Parker demanded that the newspaper and the TV show send formal apologies to Elvis and to him.

In 1956, Sun Studios owner Sam Phillips bought popular Memphis disc jockey Dewey Phillips a Polaroid camera for a Christmas present. When Elvis saw the camera, he borrowed it several times and eventually did not return it. Dewey never saw the camera again.

Several days before Christmas in 1957, Elvis was driving around Memphis in his new Cadillac, doing some last minute Christmas shopping, when he noticed one of his cousins coming out of a store. He was carrying several bags and seemed to be rushed. Elvis pulled his car over and honked his horn. His cousin came over, shook Elvis's hand, and wished him a Merry Christmas. Elvis, touched by his cousin's kind words, pulled out a $50 bill and handed it to him with orders to enjoy the holiday. Surprised by Elvis's quick and generous gesture, the cousin did not immediately notice Elvis pulling away from the curb. He yelled after Elvis,"Merry Christmas, Elvis, and thank you!"

Elvis and his girlfriend June Juanico, who was from Biloxi, Mississippi, drifted apart sometime in the fall of 1956. Elvis was always on tour, and he and June weren't able to see each other very much. June thought that Elvis was just busy, and she didn't know that he had decided to end their relationship. When the Christmas holidays came around, June was mortified to read about Elvis spending the holiday with Dorothy Harmony and Natalie Wood. When Christmas Day came, Elvis called June and casually wished her and her family a Merry Christmas and a Happy New Year and then hung up, saying he had to go. June was upset that Christmas because she and Elvis had discussed wedding plans and she thought that this would be their first Christmas as an engaged couple.

When Elvis invited Las Vegas dancer Dorothy Harmony to his Audubon Drive home for Christmas in 1956, she was ecstatic. She liked Elvis a lot and knew that Christmas was a very important time in his life. Her flight from Las Vegas to Memphis was delayed, and when she finally arrived at the airport no one was there to meet her. She decided to wait for Elvis in one of the main lounges, where she eventually fell asleep. When she woke, she was surrounded by a mob of young girls who were yelling and carrying signs which read, "Go home, Dottie Harmony!" Dorothy was horrified. The girls had found out about her plans to spend Christmas with Elvis and had come to the airport to scare her away. They did not like her or the fact that Elvis wanted to spend the holidays with her. When Elvis finally arrived at the airport, he scolded his fans for treating his friend so poorly and told them to go home. He then gently picked Dorothy up and carried her to his waiting limousine. Elvis also extended an invitation to Dorothy's parents, Mr. & Mrs. Charles Harmony, to spend Christmas with him and his family that year. The Harmonys traveled from Brooklyn, New York, to Memphis via train and they enjoyed the holiday immensely.

Two days before Christmas in 1956, Elvis and Dorothy Harmony went to Goldsmith's Department Store located at 123 Main Street to finish their Christmas shopping. They separated once inside the store. An hour or so later, Dorothy had finished her shopping and went to look for Elvis, but she could not find him anywhere. What she did not know was that news of Elvis's whereabouts had traveled quickly throughout the store and he had been forced to leave before being mobbed. He caught a cab back to Graceland and sent two of his men back for Dorothy. She had gone outside to look for Elvis and as she started to walk back into the store, one of Elvis's Cadillacs pulled up. The driver honked and motioned for her to get in. Elvis later apologized to Dorothy and bestowed a lavish display of attention upon her, kissing and hugging her in front of their parents, which made Dorothy blush.

The day before Christmas in 1956, Elvis took Dorothy Harmony to a local pet store in Memphis, where he purchased a monkey. He named the monkey "Jimbo" and paid the owner in cash. On the way back to Elvis's house, Jimbo pooped all over both Dorothy and the car. Dorothy's new outfit, a white dress with a red leather coat, was ruined. Elvis drove to the nearest gas station and had Dorothy take Jimbo to the ladies' room to get cleaned up. Meanwhile, Elvis cleaned the mess from his white leather upholstery, all the while cursing the monkey for making his Christmas with Dorothy a memorable one.

In 1957, disc jockey Dick Whittinghill from KMPW Radio in Los Angeles, California, banned Elvis' Christmas Album, stating that it was inappropriate. He denounced it over the air, saying, "It's like having Tempest Storm [a famous stripper of the 50's] give Christmas gifts to my kids!"

In the 1950's Elvis did most of his Christmas shopping at Goldsmith's Department Store, located at 123 Main Street in Memphis. By 1957, Elvis had become so popular and recognizable that he was constantly mobbed by fans as he tried to shop. Elvis made arrangements with the store owners and managers to shop after store hours.

During the Christmas holidays in 1957, Elvis came up with a scheme to test his friends and family to assure himself that he could trust those around him. He had his father, Vernon, go to the bank and bring him $15,000 in one-thousand-dollar bills. Elvis then called all of his relatives and friends over to the house. As each person arrived, Elvis invited them up to his room, where the money was fanned out on the bed. Elvis then excused himself so that the person would be left alone in the room. After several minutes, Elvis came back in, pretended that he had forgotten why he called the person up to his room, and asked them to leave. After each person left, Elvis quickly counted the money. After doing this several times, Elvis found one bill missing and immediately confronted the thief. According to Elvis, the person turned out to be one of his cousins. After this incident, Elvis warned everyone in his trust not to mention his business in front of this cousin and not to allow him back inside his group. Elvis was very hurt that Christmas, knowing that a member of his own family had stolen from him.

Promotional concert poster of Elvis's appearance at The Yule Tide Jamboree and Dance—Cook's Hoedown, December 28, 1954.

Christmas ornament, 1990's.

Elvis at the Louisiana Hayride in Shreveport, Louisiana, on December 16, 1956.

Being interviewed at the Louisiana Hayride in Shreveport, Louisiana, on December 16, 1956.

Also being interviewed at the Louisiana Hayride in Shreveport, Louisiana, on December 16, 1956.

At the Louisiana Hayride in Shreveport, Louisiana, December 16, 1956.

Beautiful Christmas greeting card.

Inside the Christmas greeting card.

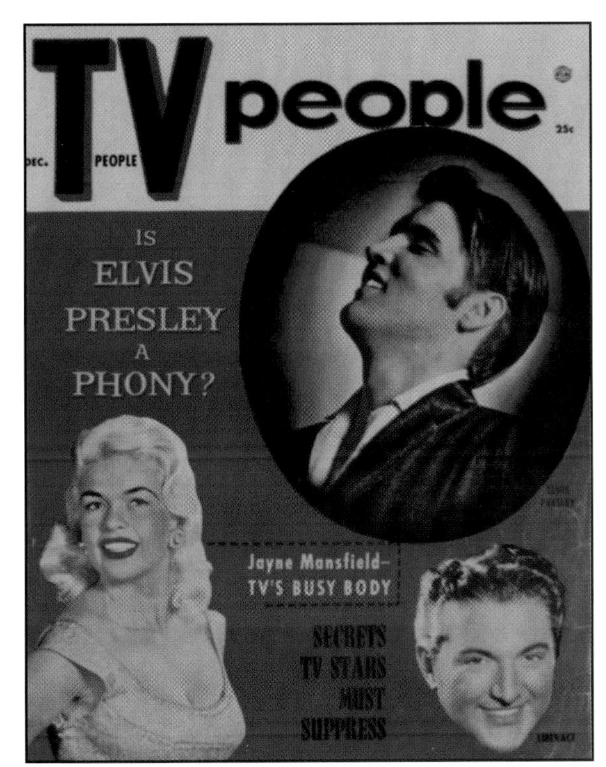

TV People *magazine, December 1956.*

Christmas greeting card from Great Britain.

Elvis posing for photographers hired by the Colonel. 1957 was Elvis's first Christmas at Graceland, and the Colonel wanted to publicize the event.

Christmas greeting card.

1997 Hallmark Christmas button promoting Elvis ornaments.

Holding a personalized gift, Elvis poses for photographers at Graceland, Christmas 1957.

Fan club Christmas greeting card.

Elvis and Kathy Gabriel, Miss Ohio 1957, share a touching moment near Elvis's Christmas tree at Graceland. Christmas 1957.

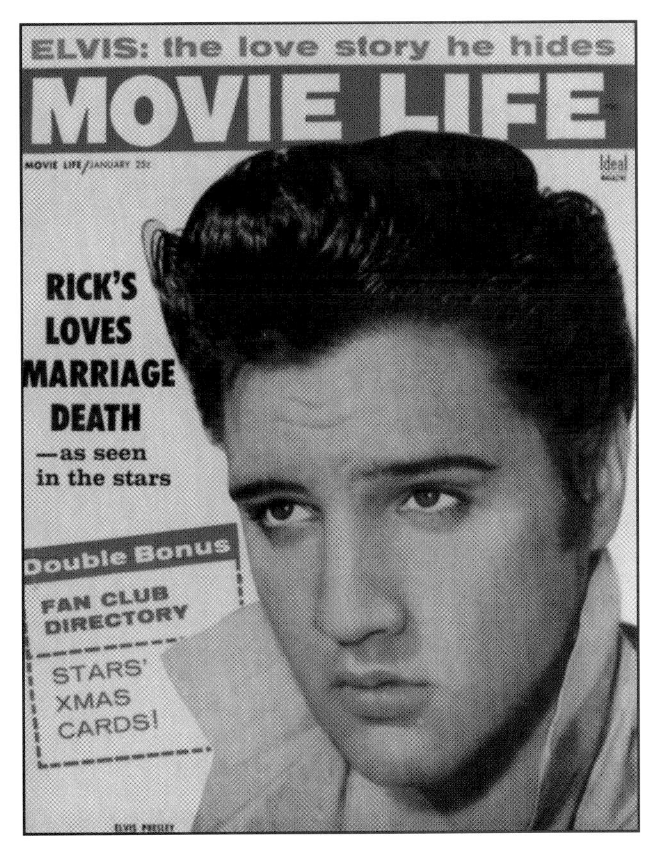

Movie Life *magazine, January 1959.*

Christmas ornament by Classic Collector's Series, 1990's.

Photo Christmas greeting card from a fan club.

Inside the February 1960 Movieland & TV Time *magazine. Includes autographed photo of Elvis and story, "The Gift From Elvis That Came After Christmas."*

Very rare Christmas card from Elvis and the Colonel, 1957 (RCA).
This actual card was sent by Elvis personally and was postmarked in Memphis on December 20, 1957.

RCA Christmas postcard from 1958.

Chapter 4
A Soldier's Christmas

On December 18, 1957, Elvis received a Christmas present from the US Army: his draft notice. It was delivered to Graceland by Milton Bowers, head of the Memphis Selective Service Commission. The notice read: "Greetings! You are hereby ordered for induction into the armed forces of the United States and to report to room 215, 198 South Main Street, Memphis, Tennessee at 7:45 A.M., on the 20th of January for forwarding to an armed forces induction station." Elvis's draft card number was 40-86-35-168.

Shortly before Christmas in 1957, representatives from the US Army, Navy, and Air Force approached Elvis with special offers, hoping he would choose their service branch. The Air Force promised Elvis a singing ambassadorship and a position as an assistant recruiting officer. The Navy offered Elvis the opportunity to perform during his free time, an admiral's housing facility, and his own private unit made up of his Memphis friends. The Army tried to entice Elvis with a position in the special services which would allow him to tour bases around the world. He would also be allowed to record and to make personal appearances whenever he desired. After consulting with the Colonel and his parents, Elvis ultimately decided to join the Army. While in the service, however, he turned down all offers for special services in which he was to perform. He wanted to be treated like all the other men in his platoon, and this attitude won him the respect of his fellow soldiers.

Before Elvis entered the Army, the Colonel had special Christmas cards printed up from the two of them. They were sent to the people they worked with as well as to fans and family members. The Colonel wanted everyone to remember this occasion as Elvis entered the Army. The inside of the card read: "For a cool Yule and a frantic first!"

On Christmas Eve in 1957, Elvis wrote a letter to the Memphis Draft Board, requesting a 60-day deferment on his draft. He needed the time so that he could finish filming *King Creole*. He noted that if he had to leave the picture unfinished, it would cost Twentieth Century Fox over $350,000! Elvis signed the letter, "Merry Christmas to everyone on the board."

After being sent to Germany in September 1958, Elvis missed his family a great deal. He decided to have his father and paternal grandmother, Minnie Mae Presley, join him for the Christmas holiday in Germany. Elvis remembered one of his mother's cardinal rules, the family should always be together, and he upheld this tradition long after Gladys's death. Vernon and Minnie Mae Presley stayed in Germany with Elvis until his discharge in March of 1960.

By December 8, 1958, Colonel Parker had sent out over 25,000 of his annual Christmas cards from himself and Elvis. The cards depicted the Colonel dressed up as Santa on the front. The Colonel strongly believed in the adage "out of sight; out of mind." He did not want anyone to forget about Elvis while he was away in the Army.

When Colonel Parker saw Elvis's personal Christmas cards in 1958, he liked the design and asked Elvis and Vernon how many they had printed. He was told that one million had been printed, and that Elvis was sending them to everyone he knew or had had any kind of contact with over the years. Most of the cards would be sent from Memphis, with a portion sent from Germany.

In Frankfurt, Germany, on December 20, 1958, Elvis purchased a used white BMW 507 as a Christmas present for himself. The two-seater sports car cost $3,750. The car was previously owned by German race car driver Hans Stuck, and the transaction between the two celebrities was made public. After Elvis brought the car home, he needed to change the racing engine to a touring one because he had no use for a fast engine. No other soldier could afford such a car, and no other soldier owned a car while living on the base. At the same time Elvis bought himself the BMW, he bought his father a sleek black Mercedes Benz.

A few days before Christmas in 1958, Elvis and his troop set up a Christmas tree in the main headquarters. As the men decorated the tree, Elvis's job was to make sure that it stood tall and straight. The men also had to clean their barracks and gear. They scrubbed, polished, washed, and waxed everything from the floors to the tanks, and sang Christmas carols as they worked. Elvis was given the job of cleaning the mirror in the bathroom, as the soldiers agreed that he loved to look at himself. As Elvis polished the mirror, he joked, "Aaah! Ain't I a handsome son-of-a-bitch!"

When Elvis and his unit were informed that they were being shipped out to Bremerhaven, Germany, the press was informed as well. The troop traveled from Fort Hood, Texas, to Brooklyn, New York, where they were to board the USS Randall. At the train station, one of Elvis's friends brought along Janie Wilbanks, a girl from Elvis's hometown of Tupelo. She was a classic beauty with black hair, and Elvis was smitten with her dark, sultry looks. After he was settled in Germany, Elvis sent for Janie and she spent the Christmas 1958 holiday with him. Elvis presented Janie with a beautiful turquoise ring on Christmas Day.

Christmas of 1958 was a difficult time for Elvis, as it was the first he spent without his mother. At the time, he was living at the Grunewald Hotel in Bad Nauheim, Germany, with his father, his grandmother, and his friends. Bad Nauheim was a resort town that catered primarily to older people, and Elvis had to stay within the limits of the hotel's policies. That Christmas, Elvis needed to release the pent-up frustration he felt, so he gathered his friends and they shot off Roman candles in front of the hotel. As Elvis lit the candles with his cigar, his friends scattered, looking for hiding places to protect them from the fiery balls. An hour later, Elvis went back into the hotel and started to shoot Roman candles at the people passing below. Several of the victims complained to the manager, who scolded Elvis for being so reckless and irresponsible. He threatened Elvis by saying that if he received just one more complaint from anyone about anything, he would personally escort them out of the hotel, Christmas or no Christmas!

The special holiday menu Elvis and the other troops were treated to in 1958 was served on china instead of on the typical tin trays. The menu consisted of shrimp cocktail, olives, carrots, fruit cups, sweet pickles, turkey with oyster stuffing, cranberry sauce, snowflake potatoes, candied sweet potatoes, buttered asparagus tips, whole kernel corn, Parker House rolls, pumpkin pie, coffee, salted nuts, and hard candy.

Elvis took his father with him to the Army mess hall for Christmas dinner in 1958. Elvis's grandmother, Minnie Mae Presley, was not feeling well and Elvis did not want her to go through all the work necessary to prepare a large meal. After he and his father had their fill, Elvis loaded a large container with food and delivered it to his grandmother.

Vernon Presley spent his first Christmas after the death of his wife with a woman he'd recently met named Dee Stanley. He bought sleds for her three young sons, David, Ricky and Billy. Elvis did not approve of his father showing interest in another woman so soon after Gladys's death, so he buried himself in his duties and avoided all contact with the Stanleys.

Elvis had hoped that it would snow for Christmas in 1958, but it did not snow until New Year's Eve. When Elvis saw the white flakes falling, he dressed quickly and ran outside. He relished the peaceful night and the soft dark pink sky. He felt that he was back in Memphis for a moment, standing in front of his beautiful home. When he opened his eyes, he was saddened to find himself still in Bad Nauheim. Several hours later, when the entire resort town was covered in several inches of white, Elvis and his men again ventured outside and together built their first German snowman!

In 1959, Elvis received word that, due to his good conduct dispensation, he would be discharged from the Army sometime before Christmas. He was thrilled at the prospect of spending the holiday back home at Graceland. Unfortunately, Elvis was not discharged until three months later, in March of 1960.

Sometime before Christmas in 1959, a large package was delivered to Elvis's rented house at 14 Goethestrasse. Although the package bore markings from the United States, there was no return address on the box. Elvis was highly suspicious and asked one of his men to open it while he waited in another room. The box, because of its impressive size, made Elvis wary; he imagined a person hiding inside who would attack him when the box was opened. Much to his relief, his men found a huge, fully-decorated Christmas tree inside. The sender had obviously wanted Elvis to enjoy a traditional American Christmas in Germany. Elvis loved it! He had the tree set up in a corner of the house and had his men put their gifts under it.

In 1959, a woman named Daisy Cannon was hospitalized in Evansville, Indiana. Paralyzed and bedridden, Daisy spent her days listening to Elvis songs on the radio. In the fall of 1959, her roommate, Joy Edwards, was released after a lengthy stay. The two women had become good friends and, hoping to make Daisy's Christmas a special one, Joy wrote to Elvis and explained her friend's situation. Joy knew that with Elvis serving in the Army in Germany, the chances of Daisy receiving a response from her idol were slim, so she bought Daisy a pretty floral gown as an alternate present. When Christmas came and there was no response from Elvis, Joy sent the gown to Daisy at the hospital. Several days later, Joy received a letter from Daisy, thanking her for the gift. Half way down the page, Joy read the line, "I have also received a letter from Elvis Presley! Can you believe it?" Elvis's letter contained words of comfort, hope, and friendship for Daisy, along with wishes for a Merry Christmas and a Happy New Year.

In 1959, Colonel Parker sent uncut sheets of their Christmas postcards to reporters in the United States. A note included with the postcards instructed the recipients to mail them to their friends and family for Christmas. Many of the reporters did as Parker instructed; others were angered by his newest ploy to publicize Elvis while he was in the Army and they threw the cards away.

In 1959, Elvis met Margrit Buergin, a German secretary who spoke little English. As his Christmas present to her, Elvis gave Margrit a diamond watch and a matching gold necklace and earring set. Little did Elvis know, Margrit disliked jewelry and she gave the gifts to her mother.

On Christmas Day in 1959, Elvis threw a large party for his friends and fans, his soldier buddies, and several officers at his rented home at 14 Goethestrasse in Bad Nauheim, Germany. Vernon shocked everyone by bringing Dee Stanley and her husband, Bill. Rumors were already spreading that Vernon and Dee were spending too much private time together; Elvis was not thrilled about his father lavishing his attention on Dee or any other woman, as Gladys had died only a year before. Elvis had a hard time enjoying his Christmas party, as he was trying to keep tabs on his father and Dee. He did not like their "relationship," especially since Dee was married to a highly respected US Army officer. Dee later divorced Bill and she and her three young sons moved back to the United States with Vernon. Vernon and Dee were married a short time later.

Elvis's Third Armored Division threw a special Christmas party for 115 German orphans from the Steinmuehle Orphanage in 1959. Elvis supplied the food, beverages, music, and gifts. That year, he did something he had never done before: he dressed up as Santa Claus! The orphaned children loved the party. When the children called Elvis their "foster father," Elvis began to cry. With tears rolling down his face, he hugged each child tightly, thanking them in German. Orphanage director Hermann Schaub thanked Elvis with a public speech, stating that never in the history of the orphanage had anyone treated the children so well.

To help Elvis feel at home and to show him that he was loved during his Christmas in Germany, a group of local American teenagers made a special trip to his home and sang Christmas carols in front of the house. Elvis was incredibly touched by their thoughtfulness and holiday spirit and he thanked each caroler personally. He then asked the group to join him in singing "Blue Christmas," but the teens preferred to listen to Elvis sing rather than ruin the song with their own voices.

When Elvis arrived at Graceland after being discharged from the Army on March 5, 1960, he was greeted by the sight of his mother's fully-decorated, prized white nylon Christmas tree, which had been standing in the living room for three years. Elvis had the tree stored in the attic until Christmas, at which time he again set it up downstairs. When the tree was decorated and turned on, the music and lights brought back memories of his beloved mother. He could hear her saying, "If we are careful, we can use it every Christmas, it is so beautiful." He could visualize her sitting there gazing happily at the tree. Elvis sat looking at the dancing lights and listening to the Christmas chimes playing as the tree went round and round. When "Silent Night" came on, Elvis began to cry. Blinded from the tears and barely able to see, he grabbed the tree and carried it back up to the attic. Elvis did not know when he would be able to bring the tree back down again. His mother's Christmas tree, with all its beautiful memories, remains to this day just as he left it, in the attic at Graceland.

Elvis reading the Army draft notice that was delivered by Milton Bowers. Taken December 20, 1957, at Graceland.

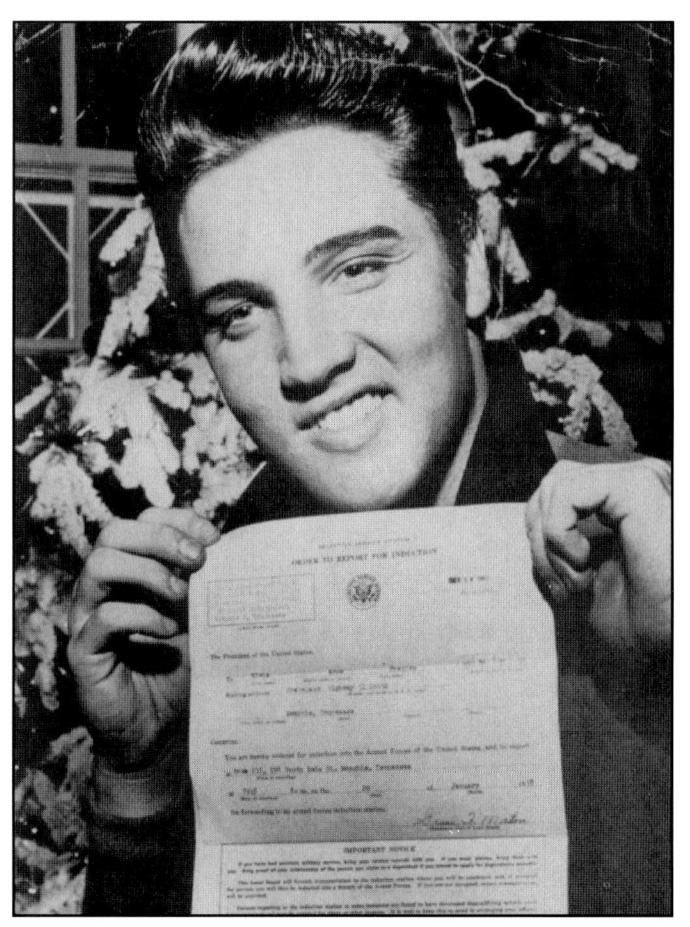

Elvis holds up his official Christmas gift from Uncle Sam—a draft notice! Photo taken at Graceland on December 20, 1957.

On December 20, 1958, Elvis bought himself a beautiful white BMW 507 from race car driver Hans Stuck for $3750. Ursula Siebert, a German model, hands Elvis the keys to the car during a public appearance in Frankfurt.

ELVIS EXTRA

NUMBER 6 Newsletter of the Elvis Presley Official Fan Club Australia FOURTH QUARTER 1993

CHRISTMAS AT GRACELAND

A special contribution from
PATSY ANDERSEN, GRACELAND

Elvis Presley led a very active life with movies, concert tours, and Vegas engagements. There was usually so much going on in his life and career. Graceland was always his private little corner of the world - a place where he could relax and be himself, away from the pressures of superstardom. It would be his favorite place to be for the next twenty years, the rest of his life.

Regardless of how hectic his schedule, Elvis was always home for Christmas (except for one year due to recording a soundtrack).

Decorating for Christmas was a big event at Graceland. The decorations usually went up soon after Thanksgiving and would remain in place at least through to his birthday on January 8th. Almost every room of the Mansion displayed the excitement of the season. Christmas trees could be found in the dining room, the living room, the den (aka the Jungle Room), and even in Elvis' bedroom. Elvis would have all the blue draperies taken down in the living room and the dining room and they would be replaced with beautiful red draperies. The red draperies, along with the gorgeous white carpeting provided these two rooms with an abundance of Christmas atmosphere. However, the dining room was the center of activity with the largest, prettiest live tree to be found in Memphis. And as with many families, the Presley's would decorate the tree together, sometimes singing Christmas songs as they worked. Elvis, however, usually did not participate in the actual decorating - he preferred to supervise, watching the others having a good time.

Outdoor decorations were elaborate as well. In 1957, Elvis had a 'Santa with a sleigh

Continued page 3

We wish you a MERRY ELVIS CHRISTMAS and a Safe, Happy and Prosperous New Year

Fan club brochure, special Christmas issue, dated 1993.

Elvis peeks out of his newly-purchased BMW. Frankfurt, Germany, December 20, 1958.

RCA Christmas postcard, 1959. Some contained a message from Elvis via Western Union.

Movie Teen Illustrated *magazine, December 1958.*

Rare fan club photo card sent in the late 1950's.

Collector's plate by Delphi, 1992. "Blue Christmas" by artist Nate Giorgio.

On March 7, 1960, Elvis was subjected to a press conference at Graceland celebrating his Army discharge. Unhappy about the conference, here Elvis sits on his desk near his Christmas tree, answering reporters' questions. (Hallmark, 1990's)

Elvis at home, March 7, 1960.

Beautiful Christmas card made by a fan club, 1994.

MEMPHIS, TENN., TUESDAY, MARCH 8, 1960

A Mansion Full of Memories

DRESSED CASUALLY in his first civilian clothing since being discharged from the Army, Elvis holds a friendly chat with newsmen in his two-room office building behind his Graceland mansion. In the corner stands his 1957 Christmas tree, still lighted. "That was my last Christmas at home," he said.

TASTY TIDBIT—Elvis samples a large white cake, baked in the form of a guitar, sent to him at Graceland by an "anonymous" fan. The cake bears the message, "Welcome Home, Elvis." On the side it says, "Hound Dog," name of one of his many million-seller records.

Elvis Plans to 'Stay Right At Home' for a Few Days

Front page of the Memphis Press Scimitar, *Tuesday, March 8, 1960.*

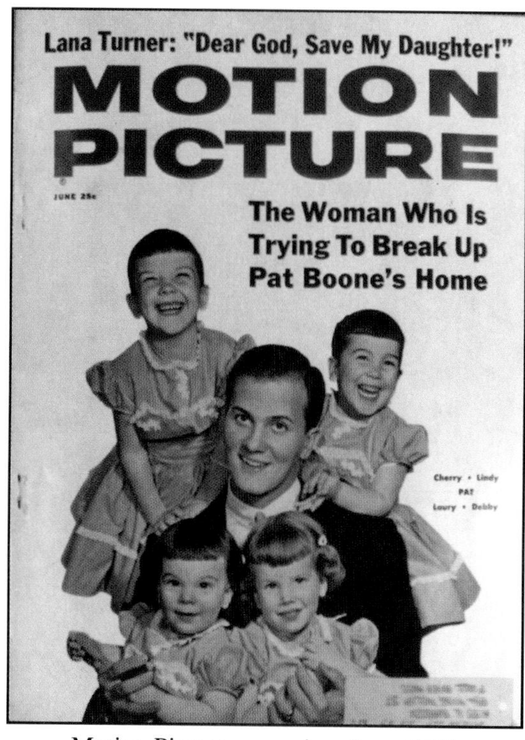

Motion Picture *magazine, June 1960.*

Full page color pinup inside Motion Picture *magazine, June 1960.*

1960 fan club Christmas greeting card.

Elvis kneeling in front of the Christmas tree that his mother had loved so much. During his post-Army discharge press conference at Graceland.

Elvis arrived at Graceland on March 7, 1960, after a two year stint in the Army. When he returned home, he was welcomed to the sight of the still-standing Christmas tree.

Elvis at Graceland after his Army discharge press conference, March 7, 1960.

Photoplay *magazine, January 1960.*

Inside Photoplay *magazine, January 1960.*
The Christmas Contest.

Inside Photoplay *magazine, January 1960.*
The Christmas Contest.

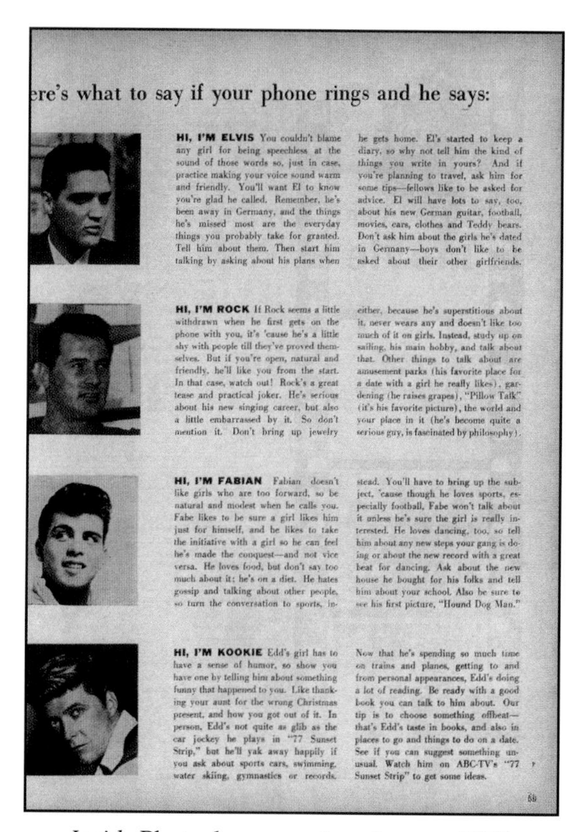

ere's what to say if your phone rings and he says:

HI, I'M ELVIS You couldn't blame any girl for being speechless at the sound of those words so, just in case, practice making your voice sound warm and friendly. You'll want El to know you're glad he called. Remember, he's been away in Germany, and the things he's missed most are the everyday things you probably take for granted. Tell him about them. Then start him talking by asking about his plans when he gets home. El's started to keep a diary, so why not tell him the kind of things you write in yours? And if you're planning to travel, ask him for some tips—fellows like to be asked for advice. El will have lots to say, too, about his new German guitar, football, movies, cars, clothes and Teddy bears. Don't ask him about the girls he's dated in Germany—boys don't like to be asked about their other girlfriends.

HI, I'M ROCK If Rock seems a little withdrawn when he first gets on the phone with you, it's 'cause he's a little shy with people till they've proved themselves. But if you're open, natural and friendly, he'll like you from the start. In that case, watch out! Rock's a great tease and practical joker. He's serious about his new singing career, but also a little embarrassed by it. So don't mention it. Don't bring up jewelry either, because he's superstitious about it, never wears any and doesn't like too much of it on girls. Instead, study up on sailing, his main hobby, and talk about that. Other things to talk about are amusement parks (his favorite place for a date with a girl he really likes), gardening (he raises grapes), "Pillow Talk" (it's his favorite picture), the world and your place in it (he's become quite a serious guy, is fascinated by philosophy).

HI, I'M FABIAN Fabian doesn't like girls who are too forward, so be natural and modest when he calls you. Fabe likes to be sure a girl likes him just for himself, and he likes to take the initiative with a girl so he can feel he's made the conquest—and not vice versa. He loves food, but don't say too much about it; he's on a diet. He hates gossip and talking about other people, so turn the conversation to sports, instead. You'll have to bring up the subject, 'cause though he loves sports, especially football, Fabe won't talk about it unless he's sure the girl is really interested. He loves dancing, too, so tell him about any new steps your gang is doing or about the new record with a great beat for dancing. Ask about the new house he bought for his folks and tell him about your school. Also be sure to see his first picture, "Hound Dog Man."

HI, I'M KOOKIE Edd's girl has to have a sense of humor, so show you have one by telling him about something funny that happened to you. Like thanking your aunt for the wrong Christmas present, and how you got out of it. In person, Edd's not quite as glib as the car jockey he plays in "77 Sunset Strip," but he'll yak away happily if you ask about sports cars, swimming, water skiing, gymnastics or records. Now that he's spending so much time on trains and planes, getting to and from personal appearances, Edd's doing a lot of reading. Be ready with a good book you can talk to him about. Our tip is to choose something offbeat—that's Edd's taste in books, and also in places to go and things to do on a date. See if you can suggest something unusual. Watch him on ABC-TV's "77 Sunset Strip" to get some ideas.

59

Inside Photoplay *magazine, January 1960.*
The Christmas Contest.

Front of card #75 of the Elvis Collection by the River Group, 1992.

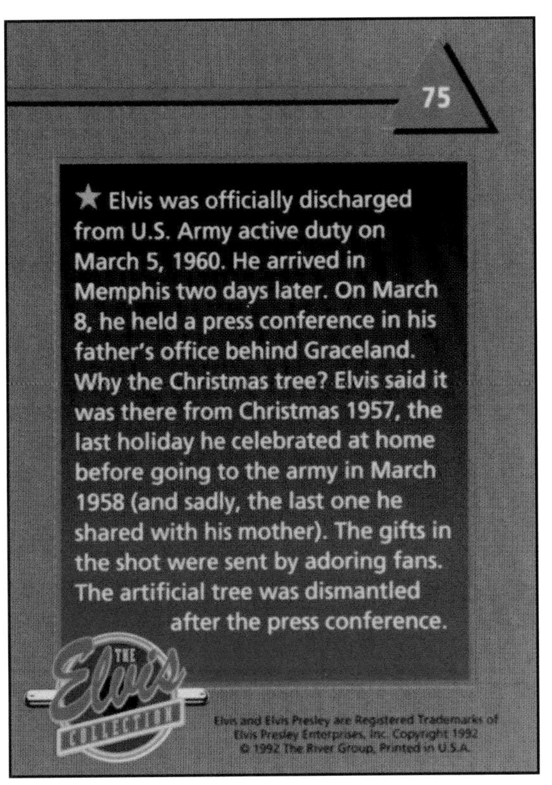

Back of card #75 of the Elvis Collection by the River Group, 1992.

Front of card #486 of the Elvis Collection by the River Group, 1993.

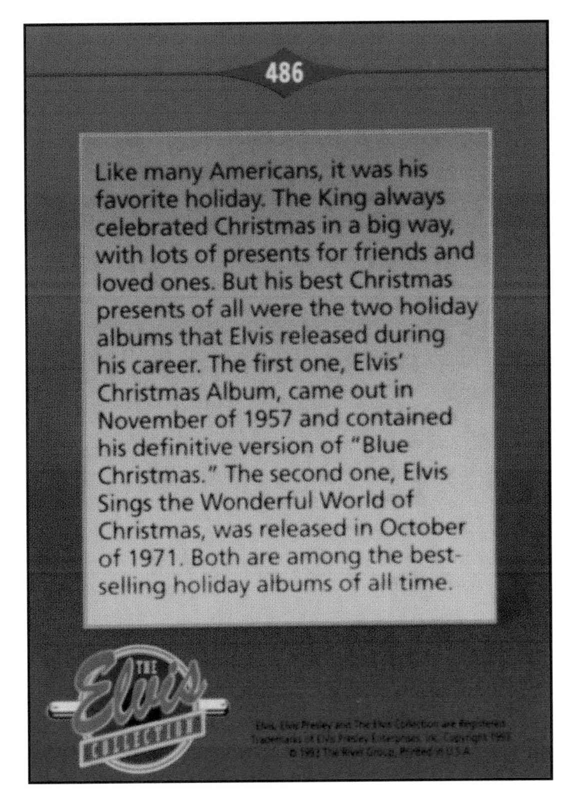

Back of card #486 of the Elvis Collection by the River Group, 1993.

Movie Teen Illustrated *magazine, December 1961.*

Fan photo greeting card.

"ELVIS WILL BE HOME FOR CHRISTMAS"

IN FARAWAY GERMANY, GRANDMOTHER PRESLEY'S CHRISTMAS DINNER WAS LIKE A PROMISE THAT SOMEDAY THEY WOULD AGAIN BE HOME FOR THE HOLIDAYS. PERHAPS THAT WILL BE SOONER THAN ELVIS DREAMED!

MY FLYING VISIT to Memphis, to Graceland, was at an end. I had gone to Tennessee to talk to those closest to Elvis, to learn what the home-folks knew about America's favorite soldier-boy that hadn't been revealed to the rest of the world, to visit Elvis' home for the first time. Now I was at the great gates of Graceland, my visit over, talking with Barnie Smith, Graceland's well known, genial guard. Suddenly something Barnie said stopped me in my tracks. "Elvis will be home for Christmas," he smiled. "At least that's what we've been given to understand. That's what we're hoping for and planning on. If he can't come, there'll sure be a lot of disappointed folks around here. But we feel pretty sure he'll make it."

Elvis will be home for Christmas! The news was cheering. I felt a sudden surge of happiness for him. Remembering what his Christmas last year and the year before were like, I thought how anxiously he must look forward to this one!

Last year he spent Christmas far from home, in Germany. Even though he was in that part of the world where so many of our Yule traditions originated—the decorated tree, countless Christmas carols, etc.—Christmas 1958 had been a lonely time for him. His friend Bobby "Red" West had written me about it. An undercurrent of melancholy ran throughout the missive. Elvis had just come back from two months of field maneuvers in the lonely, snowy wastes near the Russian border. When he came back it was only a week until Christmas. The tree in their apartment at the Gruenwald Hotel was up. "Red" and Mr Presley had decorated it. Seeing it for the first time, its lights glowing, the many gaily-wrapped parcels beneath its branches, Elvis was reminded at once of the Christmas before. That Christmas, 1957, was the last that his beloved mother had lived to see. They were (Please turn to page 62)

by DEE RYAN

Soon after Christmas, El will be discharged. He will first do a personal appearance in Australia, the TV "spec," then the movie G. I. Blues, to be released in fall of '60.

TV Movie Screen *magazine, January 1960.*

Rare Army greeting card sent by an Elvis fan club for Christmas.

1960 Christmas post card (RCA).

Chapter 5
I'll Be Home For Christmas

Elvis loved the effect of the blue lights lining airport runways, and he wanted to decorate Graceland in a similiar way. In 1960, while in Hollywood filming *Wild in the Country*, Elvis called his father and explained what he wanted done. Vernon bought hundreds of strings of blue lights and hired several electricians to carry out Elvis's instructions. The men worked for three days and finished the job just thirty minutes before Elvis arrived home for the holiday. As Elvis drove alongside the famous wall, he was speechless. The effect was so breathtaking that Elvis parked his car across the street and stared at the scene for nearly two hours. He loved how everything looked, so festive and colorful. When he finally walked inside, everyone joked with him about the lights and told him that he should now watch out for planes landing in his backyard. Elvis laughed and told them that no matter what, Graceland was the best looking place in the world and Christmas was definitely his favorite holiday!

Although filming of *Wild in the Country* was not completed by the time Christmas rolled around in 1960, Twentieth Century Fox allowed Elvis to return to Tennessee for the holiday. Elvis hated to fly, but as the schedule called for him to remain on the set until Thursday, December 22, he was forced to take a plane home to Graceland. The American Airlines flight from Los Angeles landed in Memphis at 10:00 a.m. on Friday, December 23. Elvis returned to California via bus on January 18, 1961, to complete the movie.

Elvis met his girlfriend Nancy Sharpe's family in St. Louis during the Christmas holidays in 1960. Elvis and Nancy had been dating for a while, and Elvis thought it was time to meet her family. In light of Elvis's reputation, Nancy's parents also wanted to meet Elvis to make sure they didn't have to worry about their daughter. Elvis brought Christmas presents with him for each member of her family.

Elvis spent the 1961 Christmas holiday in California, over 3,000 miles away from his Graceland home. Production of the film *Kid Galahad* had gone into overtime, which required Elvis's presence on the set. In addition, Elvis had recently broken up with his girlfriend of six years, Anita Wood. She had been secretly living at Graceland, but moved out after they broke up.

Another reason Elvis chose to spend Christmas 1961 away from Graceland was that Elvis had a hard time accepting Vernon's new love interest, Dee Stanley, and her three sons. He didn't like the fact that she had talked his father into moving out of Graceland and into a house of their own on Hermitage Street. Dee wanted to get away from Elvis and live her own life with Vernon. She thought Elvis meddled too much, and she was also tired of Elvis's ever-present Memphis Mafia and the parades of women coming in and out of the mansion.

Elvis was hurt by all of this and did not know how to react except by running and staying away. He did not want to spend the holiday knowing that he was not 'liked' by anyone, so he spent Christmas in Hollywood with his entourage and the movie crew.

One Christmas in the early 1960's, Elvis was en route to Forest Hills Cemetery at 1661 Elvis Presley Boulevard in Memphis to visit his mother's grave when he spotted a homeless man pushing a cart filled with his life's treasures. The man was selling some of his things so that he could eat. Elvis drove up to the destitute man and stuck his hand out the window of his Cadillac. When the man came over and took what was in Elvis's hand, he thanked him. Elvis then quickly drove away and called out, "Merry Christmas!" It wasn't until the man opened his hand and counted the money that he knew he had been given five $100 bills! He immediately got down on his knees and looked up at the sky, obviously thanking God for making this Christmas the best he had ever had.

On his way home from Hollywood for the 1963 Christmas holiday, Elvis decided to be the driver of his tour bus instead of relaxing while one of his men drove, which was his usual custom.

During the long and tiring trip, Elvis needed to stop. When he saw a small restaurant in the distance, he pulled into its lot. By the time they were served their food, word had spread that Elvis Presley was eating at the restaurant. A mob of a hundred or so people had gathered in front of the restaurant waiting for the famous actor and singer to emerge. Elvis nearly choked on his sandwich when he saw all those people outside. Elvis told his men to gather their sandwiches and drinks and to run like lightning to the bus and not to stop for anyone or anything. When they were ready, Elvis and his boys ran for the door. The people were so shocked by what was happening that they could not react fast enough. Before anyone knew it, Elvis was on the bus and slowly pulling out. As he exited the lot, Elvis rolled down his window and called out to everyone, "Merry Christmas!"

On December 13, 1963, Elvis bought approximately fifty tickets to the premiere of *Cleopatra* starring Elizabeth Taylor. The tickets, meant as Christmas presents for Priscilla, family, and friends, were quite a hot item at the time and tickets were hard to come by. Each ticket cost Elvis $12.50, which was very expensive for 1963. When the date of the premiere arrived, Elvis apologized to everyone and told them that he could not make the premiere. Unbeknownst to Priscilla, Elvis traveled back to Hollywood to be with Ann-Margret for several days.

Artist Betty Harper drew four hundred pictures of Elvis when she was a teen in the mid-1960's, which her father sent to Elvis at Graceland. Betty was quite embarrassed, as she intended to keep the drawings to herself, and never once thought that Elvis would see them. She hoped and prayed that Elvis would like them. As it turned out, Elvis loved Betty's drawings and in return he sent her a Christmas card every year. Today Ms. Harper is a highly respected artist. No one can capture Elvis quite like she can.

On Monday night, December 13, 1965, sixty-five nurses made a special trip to Graceland. When they spotted Elvis in his driveway sitting atop his motorcycle and chatting with his fans, they ran over and surrounded him. Elvis was shocked to see the white-clad nurses barricading him with their bodies, but laughed it off. The nurses then proceeded to serenade Elvis with Christmas carols. When Elvis heard them sing he took off his helmet in a show of respect to the ladies and listened carefully. When they sang one of his favorites, Elvis joined in. When the nurses finished their repertoire, Elvis got off his motorcycle and went to each nurse, thanked her, hugged her and kissed her on the cheek, making for a very special Christmas for all of them.

One year while in California, just prior to Christmas, Elvis saw a house lined with exquisite gold metallic trees. Elvis loved the effect they gave and when he got back to Graceland he asked his father, Vernon, to search for similar looking trees. Vernon went to Mr. Phipps, the designer of their Nativity set, and had him make the trees. Resulting from Mr. Phipps handiwork were six 8-foot gold metallic Christmas trees which were installed to line the driveway in front of Graceland. After 1967, Elvis had electricians adorn the trees with multi-colored lights. Each tree was trimmed in a different color such as red, blue, yellow, green, purple, and orange. When the trees were lit the effect was magnificent.

For Christmas 1965, Elvis did not buy the Colonel a Christmas gift nor did he call to wish him a happy holiday. Elvis was upset at the Colonel for forcing him to work on Thanksgiving instead of allowing him to go back to Graceland to be with his family and friends. To get back at his manager and at Paramount Studios, Elvis drove back to Memphis from Hollywood late on Thanksgiving Day and did not return until ten long weeks later. Filming came to a halt and the production went into overtime, causing the picture to go over budget. Parker was getting heat from Hal Wallis and the other studio heads, so he tried calling Elvis at Graceland to find out what was going on. All he got was a message from Elvis stating that he did not wish to speak with him. Parker was enraged! When Elvis finally returned to the studio ten weeks later, he ignored Colonel Parker, his director, and his producer, and all the studio heads. Once it was learned that the reason for Elvis's action had been their refusal to allow him the Thanksgiving holiday at home, you can be sure that Elvis was never again asked to work on a family holiday.

In 1968, Elvis was pleasantly surprised to be visited by Barbara Hearn, who Elvis had dated seriously from late 1955 up until he started filming *Jailhouse Rock* in 1957. Barbara was in Memphis for the Christmas holidays and stopped by Graceland to see how he was doing. She told the gate guard, Elvis's uncle, Vester Presley, who she was and to tell Elvis that she was there. Elvis sent for her immediately and had one of his men drive down to pick her up. Before she was able to ring the bell at the door, Elvis opened it and invited her in. Barbara had never seen Graceland and was amazed by its size and elegance. Elvis took her on a tour of the house. She commented that he had finally made it big enough to buy that big house on the hill that he had dreamed of. They then reminisced about the old times and talked about their once-serious relationship. Barbara then told Elvis that she was married and lived in South Africa with her husband and children. After seeing pictures of Barbara's children, Elvis asked her if she remembered the times when they talked about having their own children. Barbara nodded, saying that she did remember. The subject was getting awkward and was quickly changed by Elvis asking about her family. Barbara said that everyone was fine and that she was in town visiting for Christmas. She added that she could not stop herself from coming over to see him because it had been so long since they had seen each other. As the visit ended, she wished Elvis all the happiness in the world and a very Merry Christmas and the best New Year ever! Elvis got up, returned the same wishes, and hugged her tight. He then whispered in her ear, "I wonder how it could have been with us! I still love you!" As he opened the front door of his house, he gave her hand one last squeeze and kissed her for the last time.

Eating snow outside his Graceland home, 1960.

Elvis with RCA executive Steve Sholes at Graceland shortly after Christmas in 1960. Sholes was responsible for RCA signing Elvis.

Elvis and friends standing in the snow outside the back door of Graceland, 1960.

Vernon Presley, his mother, Minnie Mae, and his second wife, Dee Stanley, pose for photos at Graceland on Christmas morning, 1962.

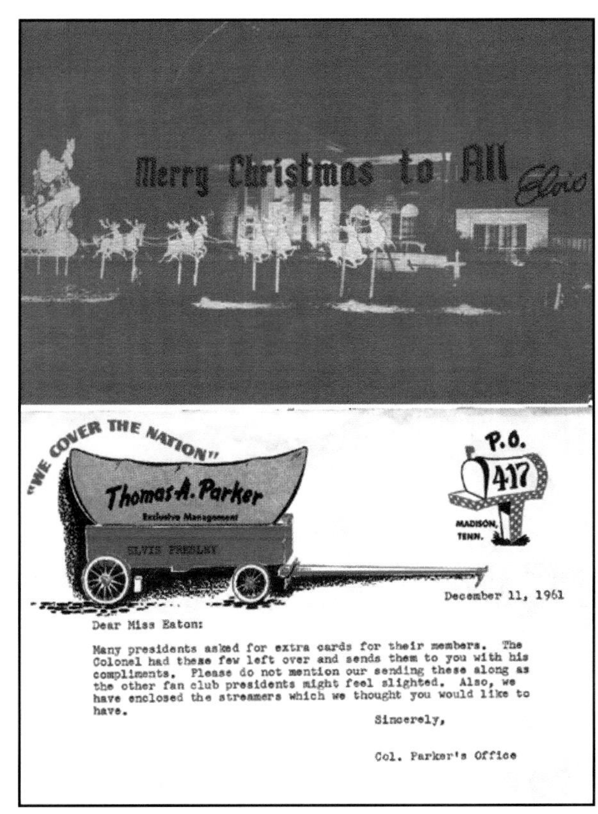

"WE COVER THE NATION"
Thomas A. Parker
Exclusive Management
ELVIS PRESLEY

P.O. 417
MADISON, TENN.

December 11, 1961

Dear Miss Eaton:

Many presidents asked for extra cards for their members. The Colonel had these few left over and sends them to you with his compliments. Please do not mention our sending these along as the other fan club presidents might feel slighted. Also, we have enclosed the streamers which we thought you would like to have.

Sincerely,

Col. Parker's Office

Blue version of the Graceland Christmas card with letter sent by the Colonel to fan clubs, December 11, 1961.

Promotional photo of Elvis from Kid Galahad. *The making of this movie caused Elvis to miss Christmas at Graceland in 1961.*

Elvis waves from his Rolls Royce parked outside Graceland, Christmas 1964.

Front view of the rare 1964 Christmas card sent out by Elvis and the Colonel.

Inside of the rare 1964 Christmas card sent out by Elvis and the Colonel.

A major construction project was underway at Graceland on Christmas morning in 1966. With several inches of snow on the ground, Elvis supervised his crew of friends in building the year's first snowman.

Everything about Elvis was flashy and unique, especially this winter coat trimmed with sequins (1966).

Front of a personal Christmas greeting card from the 1960's.

Inside of the rare, personal Christmas greeting card from the 1960's.

Elvis signs autographs for fans at Graceland several days before Christmas, 1967.

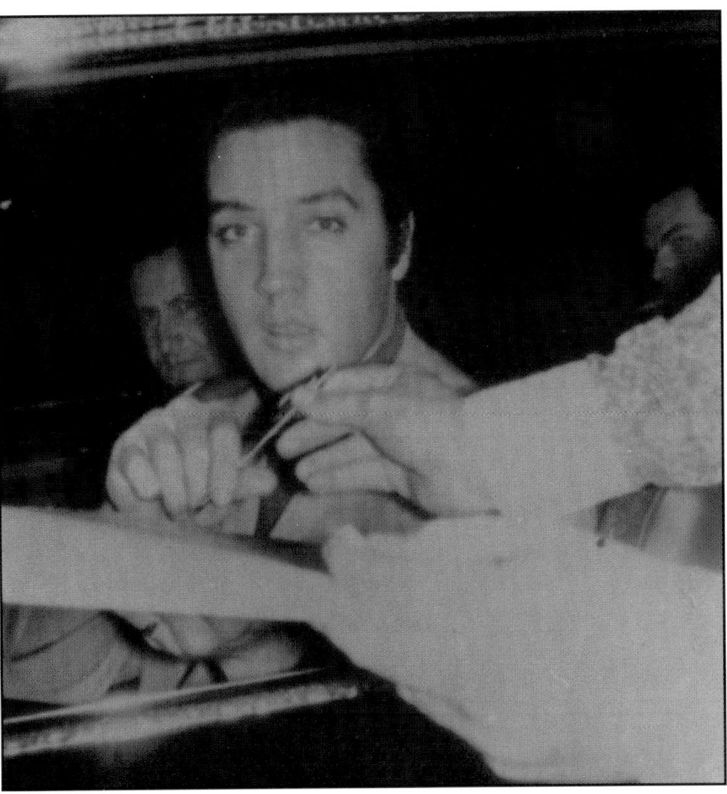

Memphis, December 9, 1967. Elvis is caught looking into a fan's camera as he finishes autographing a Christmas card for a fan.

Elvis autographs his first Christmas album for fan Virginia Coons in Bel Air, California, on December 12, 1968.

Elvis with fan Virginia Coons on December 12, 1968, in Bel Air, California.

Elvis giving out autographs outside his Bel Air, California, home on December 12, 1968.

Elvis in Bel Air, California, on December 18, 1968.

Rare, original 1964 Christmas card sent out personally by Elvis and the Colonel. Postmarked from Los Angeles, California, on December 11, 1964.

Inside the 1964 card sent out by Elvis and the Colonel.

Very rare Christmas card sent by Elvis and Priscilla in 1967, their first Christmas as husband and wife.

Inside the 1967 Christmas card sent by Elvis and Priscilla.

Chapter 6
A Christmas Romance

In 1959, Elvis threw a large Christmas party at his rented house in Bad Nauheim, Germany. Invited to the party was a fourteen-year-old American girl named Priscilla Ann Beaulieu. Elvis knew Priscilla's father, who was an Air Force officer. Priscilla, who wore an outfit borrowed from her mother for the exciting occasion, was given an 11 p.m. curfew by her parents. Elvis had lost his mother the year before and he found that Priscilla took his mind off his sorrow and seemed to fill the void in his heart.

As his Christmas gift to Priscilla in 1959, Elvis bought a beautiful platinum watch encrusted with diamonds. When Priscilla arrived at his house for the party, he called her into his bedroom, where he gave her a velvet box and told her to open it. Upon seeing the gift, Priscilla was speechless. She had never owned anything so beautiful. Before she could react, Elvis pulled her into the living room and showed all his friends his gift to Priscilla. He then put the watch on her wrist. Still in shock, all Priscilla could do was give Elvis a big hug and a kiss.

In 1960, Elvis made this statement: "I'm looking forward to spending this coming Christmas in a new way. I'm looking forward to possibly seeing some people that are gonna be shocked. I just hope they're not gonna be hurt, but I know they're gonna be shocked!" This statement was made in reference to Priscilla, the fourteen-year-old girl he had met and fallen in love with in Germany in 1959. He asked her to visit him at Graceland for the Christmas holidays, and after talking her parents into it, she was coming. Elvis knew that once his family saw Priscilla, they would be shocked that he was dating such a young girl. Elvis did not care. He loved Priscilla and wanted nothing more than to spend Christmas with her.

In 1965, Priscilla came up with a brilliant idea for a Christmas present for Elvis: a miniature car racing set. Elvis loved to play with slot cars so Priscilla thought that the set would be ideal. When Elvis opened his gift and saw what it was, he loved it. He immediately set it up in the basement and he and his men played with it for hours.

Pressured by the Colonel to 'do the right thing' and marry the young woman who had been living in his house, Elvis proposed to Priscilla on Christmas Eve morning, 1966. He called Priscilla into the bathroom, sat her up on the dresser, got down on one knee, and asked her to be his wife. Priscilla immediately said yes. Elvis Aron Presley and Priscilla Ann Beaulieu were officially engaged to be married.

During Christmas dinner, Elvis announced their engagement to his family and friends and placed a 4-star sapphire ring on Priscilla's finger. Elvis had worn the ring almost all the time in the 1950's and 1960's, as well as when they first met in Germany in 1959. The ring was sentimental to her and became a favorite of hers. Unbeknownst to his soon-to-be wife, Elvis had received that ring as a gift from sugar heiress Judy Spreckles in 1956.

Elvis's original plan concerning his marriage to Priscilla was to get married on Christmas Day 1966. He envisioned a beautiful winter wedding on the day of all days; this was the reason that he proposed to her on Christmas Eve. Elvis knew that Priscilla wanted to marry him and that she would say yes. He thought that if he asked her on Christmas Eve they could plan a quick romantic wedding in Memphis on Christmas Day. Unfortunately, Elvis never considered the incidentals that were linked with the wedding such as invitations, food, wedding dress, tuxedo, etc. Priscilla wanted her parents to be there on her wedding day and knew there was no way they could fly to Memphis with only a few hours' notice. The Colonel also said plans had to be made. Therefore the decision by Elvis, Colonel Parker, and Priscilla was to postpone the wedding until March of 1967.

On Christmas Day 1966, Elvis bought a horse for Priscilla. Elvis knew that she loved horses and had always wanted one. When Priscilla saw the beautiful Tennessee walking horse, she instantly fell in love and named him "Domino." Not wanting Priscilla to be alone when riding, Elvis bought another horse so that one of Priscilla's friends could ride with her and keep her company. Day after day, Elvis listened to Priscilla's excitement about the horse. Elvis finally had to buy one for himself. He bought a powerful palomino named 'Rising Sun' for close to $4,000 sometime after the new year.

On December 10, 1967, after having a quiet and romantic dinner, Priscilla presented Elvis with her Christmas gift. She handed him the keys and told him to look outside. Elvis went out and saw a beautiful new 1967 Cadillac Fleetwood limousine. He never imagined how beautiful a car could be until he saw this one.

Elvis presented Priscilla with a full-length black mink coat for Christmas in 1969. Priscilla was delighted that she was the owner of a mink coat. In return for her extravagant Christmas gift, Priscilla bought Elvis a beautiful black velvet suit and silk shirt. Elvis loved the suit and wore it numerous times to different functions and gatherings, including Sonny West's wedding where Elvis was the best man.

For Christmas 1971, Elvis surprised his wife with an $11,000 De Tomaso Pantera Deluxe car. Priscilla was not impressed with the sporty and exotic Ford-powered Italian sports car and told Elvis to take it back. Hurt and embarrassed, he placed ten $1,000 bills on the table in front of her and walked away. Two days later, Elvis bought Priscilla a rare Tibetan bracelet and belt set from Carrie White's Boutique in Hollywood.

It wasn't until Christmas Day in 1971 that Elvis found out about Priscilla's extra-marital affair with Mike Stone. He found out from Lisa Marie, and when he confronted Priscilla she told him that she wanted her freedom. Elvis was mortified to hear that his wife wanted a divorce. She and Lisa Marie moved out of Graceland during Christmas week, which made for a sad Christmas indeed for Elvis that year.

The latter part of 1972 was an extremely trying time for Elvis. His wife, Priscilla was seeking a divorce. Knowing that he would not have a "family" anymore, Elvis was in no mood to celebrate Christmas. He did not act like his old self. His normal Christmas routine was to go down to the gates on Christmas Day and talk with the fans for about an hour. In 1972, Elvis did not go to the gates. He also did not throw a Christmas party as he normally did, nor did he accept any invitations. In fact, he never left the house. Elvis was embarrassed about being "dumped" and was not up to the fans asking him questions about Priscilla or about what happened. His fans were disappointed and many waited for days hoping to see him, give him their gift, and wish him a Merry Christmas. But loving Elvis the way the fans did, they understood why he acted that way. To try to make him feel a little better, the fans all yelled their holiday wishes into his closed circuit TV monitors, which they knew he watched.

In 1974, it was reported that Elvis tried to talk Priscilla into coming to Graceland with Lisa Marie to spend Christmas with him. Priscilla did not want to go and told Elvis that she couldn't because she had made plans with her family. Elvis was despondent over her rejection.

For Christmas 1975, Elvis asked Priscilla if Lisa Marie could stay with him during the holidays. Priscilla, seeing that Elvis needed his daughter around him, gave him the okay. It also allowed her more time to stay in Hawaii with Mike Stone.

Fan club photo greeting card.

Rare celluloid pin button, 3.5 inches in diameter. Produced by Elvis Presley Enterprises, 1956.

Russell Stover Christmas candy, 1997.

Fan club Christmas greeting card, 1960's.

Fan club mini photo greeting card.

Elvis and Priscilla stand in front of the life-sized Nativity set at Graceland on December 10, 1965. Vester Presley, Elvis's uncle, took this photo.

Fan photo greeting card.

Fan photo greeting card.

A young Priscilla poses with her horse, Domino, which was a Christmas gift from Elvis in 1966.

Drawing of Elvis and Priscilla given to Elvis by a fan.

Fan club booklet from New Zealand.

*Fan club greeting card. Picture is from a promotional photo session in October of 1968, during which Elvis forgot to remove his wedding band. (*Trouble With Girls.*)*

From 1978, a special advertisement for the "Elvis First Cadillac Pendant." Each pendant was made of pewter and a portion of metal from Elvis's first 1956 Cadillac.

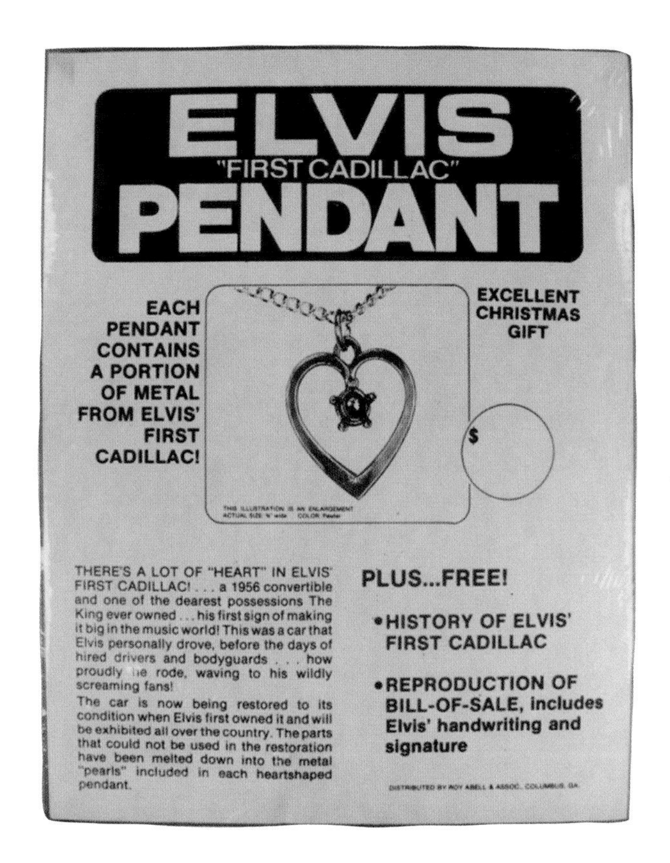

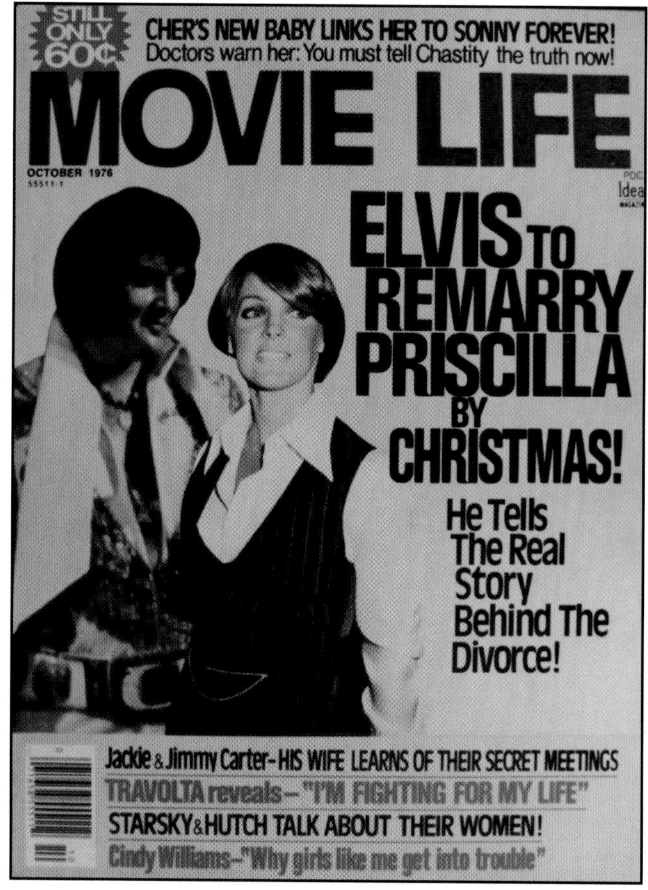

Movie Life *magazine, October 1976.*

Fan photo greeting card.

Priscilla on the cover of Modern People *magazine, January 1981.*

Back cover of Modern People *magazine.*

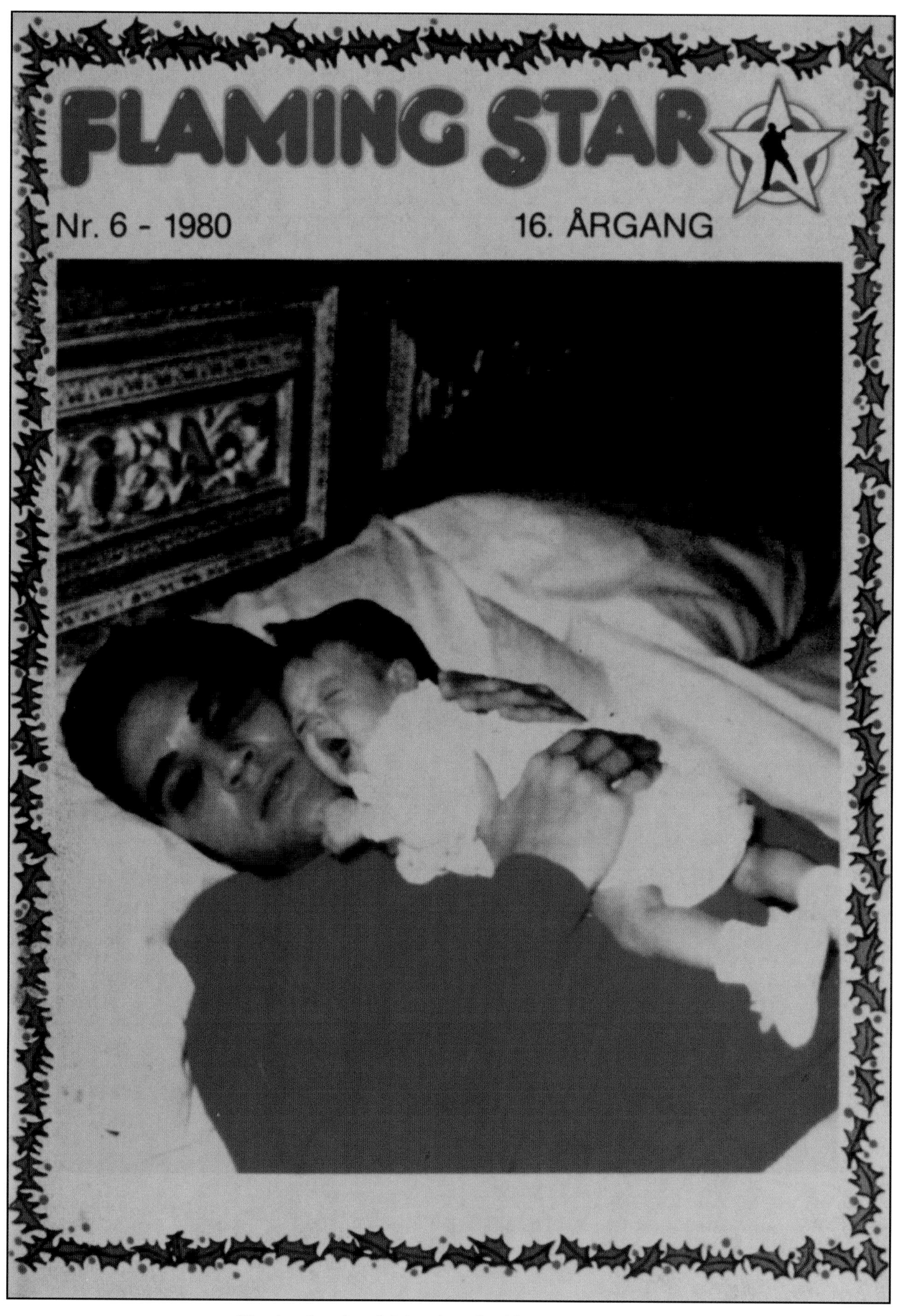

Flaming Star *fan club brochure/booklet (Norway, 1980).*

Chapter 7
Merry Christmas Baby

Elvis fans from all over the world were thrilled by the birth of his daughter on February 1, 1968. As early as September, thousands of Christmas baby gifts began arriving at Graceland for little Lisa Marie. All of Elvis's fans, worldwide, loved his first and only child and spoiled her with gifts of baby dresses, shoes, toys, stuffed animals, silver cups and spoons, and even baby tiaras. Those were from the fans who looked upon Elvis literally as a king and his daughter as a princess.

Elvis stayed up all night on Christmas Eve in 1968, wrapping gifts for his daughter. As soon as he finished, he brought Lisa Marie downstairs and let her rip open the colorful packages. Elvis got a bigger kick out of the spectacle than did Lisa Marie, who was still too young to understand what was going on.

To make her first Christmas a little more special for his new granddaughter, Vernon Presley decided to dress up as Santa Claus. Unfortunately, the unfamiliar sight of a strange man dressed in red and white scared Lisa Marie, who began crying when Vernon let out his "Ho! Ho! Ho!" Vernon sat in his designated chair and began to distribute gifts to everyone. When he got to Lisa Marie's gifts, he got closer to her and Lisa Marie cried louder and harder. Elvis went over and picked her up. Lisa Marie quickly nuzzled her head in his chest as if to hide. Elvis then asked his father to take off the costume and when Vernon did, Lisa Marie slowly peeked out from under her arm. When she saw her grandfather, she started to laugh. She then brought her arms out, begging him to take her. Lisa Marie loved her grandfather Vernon, but not as Santa Claus.

Elvis was forced to hide all of his Christmas presents for Lisa Marie because she would always find them and open them. In order to keep her from doing this, Elvis would hide her things in his private dressing room, way out of Lisa Marie's reach. On Christmas Day, after dinner and after everyone had left, Elvis put Lisa Marie's presents under the tree. In 1970, in addition to other things, Lisa Marie received a large Big Bird doll, a container of Crazy Stycks, and a Mickey Mouse gumball dispenser.

About a week before Christmas in 1976, Elvis was telling Lisa Marie about his favorite Christmases. As he recalled snowball fights and building snowmen, Lisa Marie interrupted to tell her father that she did not know what snow was. Elvis sprang into action, chartering his plane, the "Lisa Marie," and ordering the pilot to fly to an area with snow covered mountains. Once there, they landed at a nearby airport.

Elvis placed two handfuls of snow in his daughter's hands exclaiming, "That's exactly what snow is!" Lisa Marie looked up at her father and asked, "Why didn't you tell me that it was like ice?" Elvis laughed as he picked up his daughter and carried her back to the plane. This little educational trip cost Elvis $30,000!

In 1976, Elvis bought Lisa Marie her very own golf cart. Elvis had the Harley golf cart customized at the Supercycle located at 624 S. Bellevue Blvd. in Memphis. The shop sanded it down, primed it, and painted it baby blue, Lisa Marie's favorite color. Elvis had her name and a rose painted on the side. Supercycle delivered the cart to Graceland on Christmas Eve. After looking over the cart, Elvis paid the men and called Lisa Marie. As Lisa Marie ran outside, she stopped suddenly and looked at the cart. It wasn't until she read her name that she knew it was hers. She was absolutely thrilled with this gift from her father. She jumped around and kissed Elvis dozens of times. Elvis then took his daughter for a ride around the grounds and taught her how to operate the cart herself. This cart was the last Christmas present Lisa Marie would receive from her father.

Russell Stover Christmas candy, 1997.

Mini pinback button.

Plaster Christmas ornament, 1990's.

Fan photo greeting card.

Front of a Christmas greeting card by Ralph Wolfe Cowan, 1988.

Inside the Christmas greeting card.

Christmas cards by Hallmark, came in box of 20, 1996. (995 PX 4809)
Inside it reads, "Have a beautiful Christmas. Thank you very much."

Fan club crochet Christmas stocking which included a 1978 RCA pocket calendar.

Star *tabloid, December 20, 1977.*

"The Priceless Gift" souvenir copy.
Janelle McComb with Elvis in Graceland, December 1971.

The Priceless Gift

Birthdays are always special
as your fourth one comes to you
and I wondered what I'd give you
Just anything wouldn't do.

I thought of childish treasures
To hang upon your wall
Yet nothing seemed appropriate
Or none I could recall.

Money seemed so cold and fleeting
Bought treasures go so fast
And I wanted a gift to please you
And one that would also last.

You know you're sort of special
You are really all we've got
You're mama's bit of Heaven
And daddy's tiny tot.

I closed my eyes - the years rolled by
And I slowly found my way
To a shadowed corner in the attic
T'was a link to my yesterday.

I raised the lid to a frayed old trunk
And there a priceless treasure lay
A tattered apron with strings still tied
And I know I heard her say ~

"Son, I'm now just a precious memory
But dont ever forget one thing
I always tried to guide your life
With these worn out apron strings.

They guided a man named Lincoln
As he steered the Ship of State
It's the only gift I left you
That will never go out of date.

Apron strings changed the course of
History as great men felt their tug
They followed sons onto battle fields
Without the slightest shrug.

They guided both Kings and beggers
Through harmony and strife
Son, you surely must have felt their tug
For how God has blessed your life."

I bowed my head and said a prayer
For I knew God had surely touched
A tattered old trunk so tucked away
And an apron that had meant so much.

So Lisa, I give You the "Priceless Gift"
That surpasses all other things
A whole lifetime of love for you
She tied in her apron strings.

Daddy

The actual poem written by Janelle McComb.

Lisa Marie at Graceland on Christmas morning, 1973.

Elvis spends Christmas 1972 at Graceland with his two best girls: his daughter, Lisa Marie, and his new girlfriend, Linda Thompson.

Christmas at Graceland in 1972 consisted of Elvis, Lisa Marie, and Elvis's new girlfriend, Linda Thompson.

Lisa Marie sits on the floor and opens her gifts on Christmas morning, 1973.

December 1962 sticker from RCA-Victor. Used as a special giveaway from record stores who sold Elvis's Christmas records.

Lisa Marie opens her presents on Christmas morning, 1973.

Lisa Marie enjoying her own private puppet show at Graceland during Christmas 1973.

Philadelphia International Airport, June 29, 1976.

Elvis is handed a red flower along with a copy of his Christmas album at the Philadelphia International Airport on June 26, 1976.

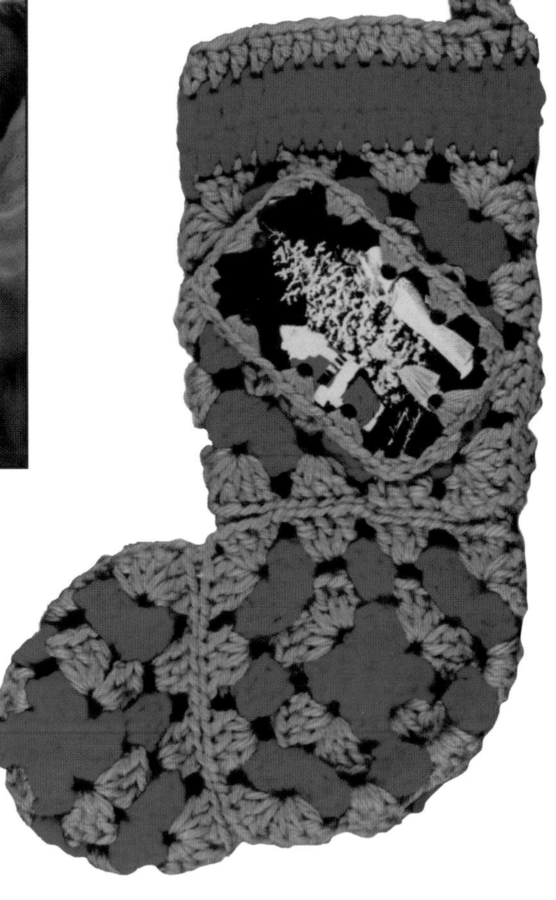

Holiday crochet stocking sold at Graceland with Elvis Christmas 1978 pocket calendar inserted in front.

Lisa Marie in the blue golf cart that Elvis gave to her for Christmas in 1976. Photo taken at Graceland in June 1977.

Lisa Marie drives her personalized golf cart around Graceland, June 1977.

Lisa Marie poses in the personalized golf cart that Elvis gave to her for Christmas in 1976. This was to become Elvis's last Christmas gift to his daughter. Photo taken at Graceland in June 1977.

Novelty tribute 45rpm record, Not Sung by Lisa Marie.

Portrait of Lisa Marie and Priscilla hanging in the dining room inside Graceland, Christmas 1988.

Bill E. Burk's

ELVIS WORLD

Dedicated To Bringing Elvis Fans Around The World Closer Together

EW #26

Our 7th Year

Welcome To Our World, Benjamin Storm Keough

Lisa Marie Presley and Danny Keough proudly show off their first son, Benjamin Storm Keough, born October 21, 1992, in Tampa, Fla. Benjamin, first grandson born to the late Elvis Presley, weighed in at 7 pounds, 8 ounces, at birth. The Keoughs' other child is Danielle, born in May 1989.
More on Page 5.

Elvis World *publication, Christmas issue (#26).*

Front cover of 32-page Singer catalog which lists all television stations which were to broadcast Elvis's comeback special, 1968.

Back cover of the 1968 RCA catalog promotoing all radio stations which would air Elvis's comeback special on NBC on December 3, 1968.

Chapter 8
A Christmas Comeback Special

For a few years, Colonel Parker sold audio tapes of Elvis singing Christmas songs and talking about the holiday under the name *The Elvis Presley Christmas Show*. After seeing how very popular the tapes were, Parker approached NBC-TV with the idea of a Christmas TV special starring Elvis. Thomas Sarnoff, Vice-President of Operations for NBC on the West Coast, liked the project. The Colonel then outlined the following terms of agreement for the special: the special should be titled either *Christmas with Elvis* or *Elvis and the Wonderful World of Christmas*; NBC would broadcast the special no more than twice at which point control would revert to Elvis and Parker; the soundtrack was to be owned by Elvis and distributed only through RCA; NBC must finance Elvis's next movie. Sarnoff agreed to the Colonel's demands and, on January 12, 1968, Parker received the go-ahead from Sarnoff via telegram.

The Colonel's right hand man, Tom Diskin, was given the assignment of finding Christmas material for Elvis to perform. Hill & Range Music Company went through their files and picked out "Jingle Bell Rock," "Little Stranger (in the Manger)," "The Voice in the Choir," and "Merry Christmas Baby." Hill & Range strongly recommended "Merry Christmas Baby" because of its bluesy sound. Since Elvis made a hit with "Reconsider Baby," the music publishing company thought that he could do the same with the Christmas song. Elvis did as was expected and recorded a marvelous version of the song.

In January 1968, Colonel Parker publicly announced that Elvis was going to do a Christmas TV special with NBC. He stated that the set would have a Christmas motif with live trees and decorations. He also said that Elvis was planning to sing twenty-four Christmas songs and would end the show with his rendition of "Silent Night" and the words, "Merry Christmas, everybody!"

The Colonel informed RCA of the possibility of another Elvis Christmas album to be called *Elvis's Christmas Album—Vol. 2*, made in conjunction with the NBC special. Excited by the prospect, RCA pushed the Singer Sewing Machine Company to sponsor the show. Singer paid $400,000 for participation in the special.

The Colonel wanted *Elvis's Christmas Special* to be lavish and classy. He envisioned having Milton Berle and Ray Bolger as guest stars, but Elvis and producer Steve Binder agreed that Berle and Bolger catered to an older, more old-fashioned audience. They were interested in something more modern. In fact, neither Elvis nor Binder was interested in doing a strictly Christmas-oriented program. The revamped program, titled simply *Elvis*, aired on December 3, 1968. Author Jim Curtin coined the phrase, *The '68 Comeback Special*, which is how the show is referred to today.

The Singer Sewing Machine Co. wanted Elvis to do a commercial while wearing one of their smocks to promote their machines, thinking their Christmas sales would skyrocket. The Colonel didn't want Elvis to do the spot but he couldn't afford to upset the sponsor of the special so, in typical Colonel Parker style, he offered Elvis's services for an exorbitant $500,000. Singer did offer $50,000, but the Colonel stood his ground. Parker feared turning Singer down in fear of them cancelling Elvis's show, which they were backing financially. To prevent any harsh feelings, he hit them with the outrageous figure, which he knew they wouldn't pay.

The Colonel, not too happy with Steve Binder for ruining his idea of an Elvis Christmas special, would saunter around the set during the show's rehearsals, chomping on his ever-present cigar and repeating loudly, "Binder, where is my Christmas music?" This would annoy Binder because Parker was interrupting his work. After a while Binder learned that the best thing to do was to ignore the Colonel, as this was the one thing that really annoyed Parker.

Knowing that he lost the fight about getting Elvis to do a Christmas special, Colonel Parker gave up the battle but not the war. He wanted Elvis to at least end the show with a Christmas song and then turn to the camera and say, "Merry Christmas, everybody!" Parker then suggested that, as the credits ran, snowflakes should slowly fall. Steve Binder said no to Parker and his crazy Christmas dreams. Parker and Binder argued about this until the first day of taping.

Despite Steve Binder's insistence that there would be no Christmas music on the Elvis special, the producer did have Elvis record "I'll Be Home for Christmas" and tentatively listed it as the last song. In the meantime, songwriters William Goldenberg and W. Earl Brown wrote the song, "If I Can Dream," and it was chosen to be the final number for the special. When the Colonel heard the tune, he exclaimed, "Over my dead body will that song be included in the show! It will not, and I repeat, it will not be chosen over a Christmas song! No way!" Elvis was unsure of what to do, but finally decided to perform the song. He told Binder, "To hell with the Colonel and his Christmas special. It's my special and I want this song as my closing number!"

Colonel Parker finally gave in to Steve Binder, agreeing that Elvis would end the show with a song not related to Christmas, but he did not want "If I Can Dream" to be the song. He suggested a religious song, "I Believe," which Elvis had recorded in 1957. Binder again said no. The Colonel was so upset about Binder trying to completely eliminate Christmas from Elvis's special that he called Tom Sarnoff, Vice-President of Operations at NBC, and complained. Sarnoff listened to Parker rant and rave for over an hour before deciding to call an emergency meeting between himself, Parker, and Binder. After hearing everything, Sarnoff decided to postpone his decision for several days, making both men wait. The following day, Binder called for a meeting which included executives from both NBC and RCA. He had Elvis perform "If I Can Dream," which delighted all those in attendance. The Colonel had been outwitted. There would be no Christmas special and no Christmas song.

Throughout rehearsals for his special, Elvis was understandably frustrated by Parker's insistence that a Christmas song be included. To lighten the mood, writers Chris Beard and Allan Blye wrote a parody of the tune "It Hurts Me" with the song ending, "They promised me sure, if I would give in / That I would, that I would, never go wrong, / But tell me the truth, is it too much to ask / For one lousy, tired ol' Christmas song?"

In order to make the Colonel happy, Elvis started to sing "Santa Claus is Back in Town," during the taping of the *'68 Comeback Special*. Before he began, he turned to the audience and said, "This being the time of year it is, I'd like to sing my favorite Christmas song." Elvis managed to sing just two lines before he stopped. "I forgot the words!" he said, with much embarrassment. He then opted to hum a portion of his own "Blue Christmas."

The *One Night With You* program, which is the unedited version of Elvis's *68 Comeback Special* shows Elvis reading his production lists to the audience. As he reaches the portion of the list which refers to Christmas, he pronounces the word as "Xmas" and "Chrithma." He repeats this several times while the audience laughs.

Inside two-page ad for Elvis's Singer special in the 1968 television listings catalog.

Fan club publication, December 1988.

Promotional advertising card printed by the Singer Sewing Machine company and distributed to customers. The front is show here; the back was a promotion for Singer sewing machines. (1968)

1968 RCA photo catalog promoting Elvis's 1968 Comeback Special.

Fan photo greeting card.

Front of card #401 of the Elvis Collection
by the River Group, 1992.

Fan photo greeting card.

401

In January of 1968, Colonel Tom Parker announced that Elvis would do a one-hour special for the NBC television network to be broadcast during the Christmas holidays. The Colonel's idea was to have Elvis sing an hour's worth of Christmas songs, a la Perry Como or Andy Williams, that could also be released as a holiday album. Fortunately, for us and for Elvis, someone else had a better idea.

THE Elvis COLLECTION

Back of card #401 of the Elvis Collection
by the River Group, 1992.

RCA pocket calendar, 1970.

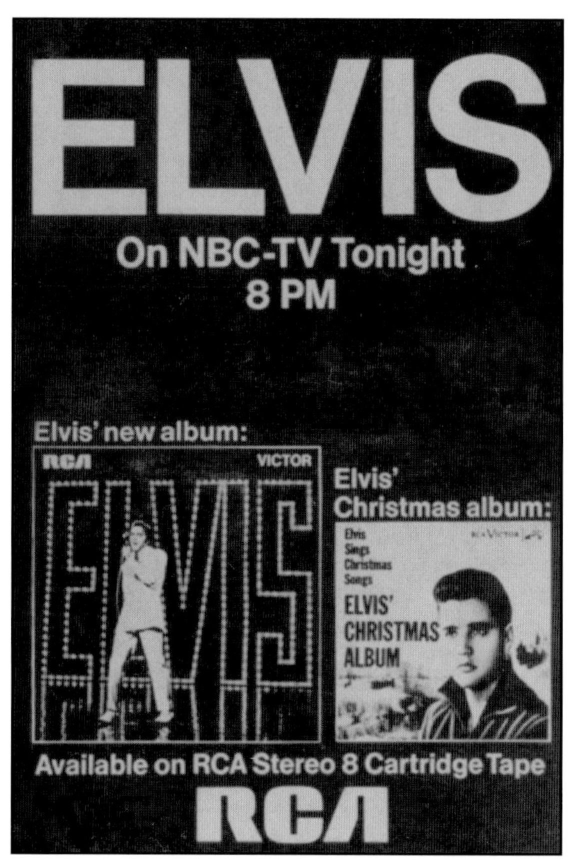

TV Guide *ad for Elvis's albums.*

RCA postcard.

Front of card #380 of the Elvis Collection by the River Group, 1992.

Back of card #380 of the Elvis Collection by the River Group, 1992.

Elvis Christmas decanter by McCormick Distilling Co.

Box to the Elvis Christmas decanter by McCormick Distilling Co.

Christmas photo greeting card from the Elvis Presley fan club of the Capital district.

Chapter 9
If Everyday Was Like Christmas

In the 1940's, Elvis received a candy bar as a Christmas present from his cousin Harold Loyd. Both families were extremely poor and the candy bar was the only present that Harold could afford. Elvis was saddened that he couldn't return the favor. The giving of this gift turned into a tradition which lasted for many years. Every Christmas, Elvis would receive a candy bar from his cousin, which served as a symbol of their hard lives in Tupelo.

As a pre-teen Elvis got a king-sized peppermint candy cane for Christmas from the mother of one of his friends who worked at the Thomas Candy Company in Tupelo, Mississippi. During those years, peppermint was expensive. After eating about half of it, Elvis took it home and shared the rest with his mother.

In 1952, Elvis dated a girl named Billie Wardlow whose family lived in the same apartment complex as the Presleys. For their first Christmas together, Elvis saved his money for several weeks to buy Billie a box of fresh cherries. When Billie opened the gift, she was delighted. She and Elvis ate half the box that Christmas Day.

On Christmas Day 1954, Elvis drove over to his girlfriend Dixie Locke's house. He went there to spend some time with her family and to give her a Christmas gift. Elvis bought her a pretty pink suit that consisted of a blouse and shorts. Dixie was surprised that Elvis had such good taste and told him that she loved the outfit. Later that evening, Elvis and Dixie went to his house to finish celebrating Christmas with Elvis's family.

Just before the Christmas holidays in 1955, Elvis made a special trip to his alma mater, L.C. Humes High School, to see Mrs. Mildred Scrivener, one of his favorite teachers. When Elvis walked into her classroom she was correcting some papers. She was surprised to see him. Elvis hugged her and gave her a Christmas gift: an electric alarm clock. Mrs. Scrivener loved the clock and thanked Elvis for it. They then reminisced about his days at school and laughed about how hard it had been for her to get him up to sing to the class. She told him that she never would have guessed that he would become a professional singer because he had always been so shy. She then told him that she was proud of him. He said that if it hadn't been for her, he might never have gotten over his shyness and would have never been able to sing in public. Just before leaving, Elvis hugged Mrs. Scrivener and wished her a very Merry Christmas and a wonderful New Year.

In 1956, Elvis gave his grandmother, Minnie Mae Presley, a hot plate for Christmas. He thought it was a great gift, since it would allow her food to stay warm when she was in her room watching television. When Minnie Mae opened

Elvis's gift, she yelled at him! She said that she would rather have had money for Christmas. Elvis, not knowing what to do or how to react to her anger, ran upstairs to his bedroom, where he pulled out several $100 bills. With money in hand, he ran back down to his grandmother's room and proudly handed her the money. More angry than she was before, Minnie Mae stood up and began screaming at the top of her lungs, "If I have to ask for money, then I don't want it!" Elvis, embarrassed, was afraid that everyone would hear her. Minnie Mae then threw the money on the floor. Elvis stormed out of her room and ran upstairs to his own, leaving the money on the floor.

One year, The Blue Moon Boys gave Elvis special plaques for Christmas. They did not know what to get a person who liked the jive style, which was something they knew nothing about. They figured that the plaques were unique and from the heart. Elvis appreciated the gifts and said that he liked them a lot.

Several newspapers ran a short announcement about "The Gift of the Year" for Christmas in 1956. The gift named was Elvis's first album, *Elvis Presley* (LPM-1254). One recipient of this great gift was Police Chief Elmer Jansen, a professed Elvis hater!

On Christmas morning in 1956, Elvis gave Dorothy Harmony a wristwatch, a turquoise portable radio and a stuffed animal. In return, Dorothy gave Elvis a St. Christopher medallion. St. Christopher is the patron saint of traveling, and Dorothy wanted Elvis to be "watched over," while he traveled.

In December 1956, a fan magazine offered Dorothy Harmony $2,500 for an interview about her first date with Elvis. Dorothy refused the offer, stating that what was between her and Elvis was private and personal and would remain that way.

When Elvis heard about her refusal, he was proud. For Christmas, he gave her a beautiful miniature toy poodle which he named Lady Gallant in honor of her loyalty. Dorothy loved the poodle's name more than the poodle itself and was happy that she had turned the magazine down. She also received an expensive white cashmere scarf from Elvis that year.

One of Elvis's girlfriends, Barbara Hearn, presented Elvis with a gold lamé vest for Christmas in 1956. The vest was lined with black satin, had gold buttons engraved with Elvis's initials, and came with a matching gold mesh belt. Elvis liked it so much that he chose to wear it for his January 6, 1957, appearance on *The Ed Sullivan Show* when he sang "Don't Be Cruel."

Elvis gave Barbara Hearn a Sunbeam electric razor for Christmas in 1956. When Barbara opened the little box she was very disappointed, as she had expected an engagement ring from him. They had been discussing marriage and children and Barbara thought that Elvis was ready to settle down. Her dreams were shattered that Christmas, which turned out to be their last together.

In 1957, Elvis decided to throw a pre-Christmas roller-skating party at the Rainbow Skate Rink located at 2881 Lamar Avenue in Memphis. By the time he returned home from the party it was three o'clock in the morning. As he drove his car past the gates, Elvis's Uncle Travis, the gate guard, asked him to come into the guard house. There, asleep on the floor, was a young girl. Uncle Travis said that she had been waiting for him for several hours. She had run out of money and could not get back home for Christmas. She had nowhere to go and nowhere to stay and decided to see Elvis.

Elvis pulled out his money and peeled off several large bills, giving them to his uncle with strict orders to give it to the girl when she woke up. When the young girl awoke two hours later, Travis presented her with Elvis's Christmas gift. The girl did not know whether to cry because she missed seeing Elvis or shout in thanks to the man who cared enough to help someone he didn't even know.

It was reported that the girl wrote Elvis a note of thanks for making her Christmas one of the best ever.

On December 18, 1957, Elvis bought Colonel Parker a tiny red Isetta sports car which cost $1,800. By the time Elvis arrived at Parker's home in Madison, Tennessee, to deliver the gift, the press had gotten wind of the visit and were on the scene. To appease both Elvis and the press, the Colonel squeezed into the car. Elvis said, "It's only a small, small way of showing my feelings for you!" Parker never drove the car, but he did use it for a mini-exhibit during the Christmas holiday in 1961. Money raised from the exhibit reportedly went to charity.

On Christmas Eve in 1957, Elvis made a special visit to Gary Pepper's house. Pepper, who had cerebral palsy, was one of Elvis's greatest fans. Elvis presented him with a crisp $1,000 bill, which Pepper proudly showed to everyone he knew. He did not spend the money until his health took a turn for the worse and he was forced to use it. Pepper went on to start the Tankers Fan Club in honor of Elvis in 1958. In 1966, Elvis presented Gary with a yellow Chevy Impala convertible. He knew that the Peppers' car was old and constantly in need of repair. Gary kept the car until the day he died.

Billy and Bobby Smith, Elvis's cousins, had their most memorable Christmas with Elvis in 1957. This was the year that Elvis gave each of them $200 in cash as his Christmas present to them. The boys were shocked, as they had never seen so much money before. Elvis got a kick out of their reactions to the money, as both Billy and Bobby hugged Elvis for making them rich! Billy and Bobby were each getting a dollar a week allowance from their parents and this was almost four years' worth of allowances all at once!

1957 was the year Elvis received the highest number of Christmas gifts from his fans. The gifts included bed spreads, clocks, jewelry, shirts, knickknacks, personalized handkerchiefs, stained glass, silver trinkets, wood carvings, framed photos of himself as well as other stars, and many photos of hopeful young girls who dreamed of being his girlfriend. When there were particular items Elvis could not use, he passed them on to charities, the homeless, the sick, and the poor.

During the Christmas holidays in 1957, Elvis asked his father to go to the bank and get ten $100 bills and twenty $1,000 bills. He then gave the money to his staff at Graceland. The majority of those who received the money then quit their jobs! Elvis was so upset by this turn of events that he lost his holiday spirit. He canceled his annual Christmas dinner and gift opening ceremony and spent a quiet Christmas with his family.

When the holidays passed and all the money had been spent, each person asked for their old job back. Elvis took them back because he knew they had families to support, but he never trusted them again. He felt betrayed by members of his family and by his employees.

In either 1957 or 1958, Elvis visited bodyguard Alan Fortas' Uncle Abe, who had to spend the Christmas holiday in the hospital. Mr. Fortas, who served as a justice on the Supreme Court, was both surprised and delighted to see Elvis and his friends arrive with balloons and gifts in tow. In addition to the small party, Elvis presented Mr. Fortas with a gold pocket watch. Mr. Fortas loved the watch and Alan always loved Elvis for being so nice to his sick uncle.

In 1958, Elvis sent a special Christmas cable to a thirteen-year-old girl stricken with polio. He found out about the girl through a newspaper and wanted to do something to brighten her holiday. At the time Elvis was involved with promoting the March of Dimes, and the sick young children touched his heart. There was nothing he wouldn't do to make them happy.

In 1959, Elvis received a Christmas gift from his entourage. It was a large trophy with the following engraving: "To Elvis, our most valuable player—from the Bad Nauheim Sunday Afternoon Football Association." When Elvis saw that the trophy was his gift, he was flabbergasted. Elvis later told several people that he had never received such a dumb gift. He was surprised that his entourage thought so little of him. Elvis said that it seemed as if they wanted to get his gift over and done with and not have to think about it anymore. Elvis was very disappointed in his friends that Christmas.

After Elvis was discharged from the service, Vernon married Dee Stanley. Upon returning to the U.S., Vernon and his new family moved into Graceland with Elvis. Elvis was not too keen about his father remarrying so soon after his mother's death, and he kept a cool distance from all of them.

When the Christmas holidays arrived in 1960, Vernon approached his son and asked him to be 'nice' to the young Stanley boys whether he liked it or not, because they were now his step-brothers. Elvis considered his father's request throughout the next week and, as Christmas Day neared, he made up his mind. As much as he hated the fact that Vernon had another family Elvis could not hold anything against the young boys. He bought various musical instruments for the boys: David got an SG Gibson guitar; Billy a bass guitar; and Ricky a set of drums. Along with the instruments, Elvis bought amplifiers, wires, microphones, and lots of music books—enough for the boys to start their own band. Elvis also bought each of them a bicycle. The Stanley boys were ecstatic. They jumped and squealed for joy. They ran over to Elvis and jumped all over him, thanking him over and over.

Elvis dated his Twentieth Century Fox movie studio wardrobe girl, Nancy Sharpe, during the filming of *Wild in the Country* in 1960. For Christmas, Elvis bought her an elaborate jewel-adorned music box. Sitting atop the box was a miniature ballerina who danced to the chimes of "I Love You Truly." This was Elvis's way of telling Nancy that he loved her without actually coming out and saying it.

Elvis was loved by millions of people and by thousands of organizations throughout the world. Many of these groups wanted Elvis to be a part of their organization for pure publicity, but some wanted to honor him for his achievements. One such organization, the Los Angeles Indian Tribal Council, loved Elvis's portrayal of a half-breed Indian in the movie *Flaming Star*. They wanted to make him a blood brother of the LA Indian community, which was a very big honor. Up until that time, the only way anyone could become a member was if he or she were full-blooded Indian and a distinguished member of the community. Elvis was known worldwide and he was bringing attention to the forgotten and abused Indian race. In honor of his contribution, on December 27, 1960, Chief Wah-Nee-Ota, the leader of the Council, presented Elvis with a chief's bonnet as their tribute to him and his contribution to their cause.

In December 1961, Elvis learned that one of his young fans, seven-year-old Debbie Fisher, had been hospitalized with a gangrenous leg and was spending her days listening to his records and looking at his pictures. He decided to do what he could to lift her spirits. On December 17, she received a box from Elvis which included an autographed jacket, twelve 8x10 glossy photos, *Elvis's Christmas Album*, an autographed photo, a belt, a pocketbook, a 2-ounce bottle of his Teddy Bear perfume, an Australian teddy bear, and a 16x20 autographed photo which read, "To Debbie, with all my best wishes. Your friend, Elvis Presley." Elvis attempted to call her, but couldn't get through as she was undergoing treatment at the time. Instead, he had the Colonel send her all of the records she needed to complete Elvis collection.

On Christmas Day in 1961, Elvis presented Colonel Parker with a brand new Lincoln Continental. The Colonel refused to accept the gift at first, insisting that he see the paperwork regarding the tax information. When he discovered that the taxes had not been paid, he sent the vehicle back to Elvis. Only when the taxes were paid would the Colonel accept the car, which he claimed was now a pure gift with no strings attached.

A young teenage girl named Elaine wrote Elvis many letters in 1961. With her letters Elaine sent Elvis little personal momentos such as ribbons, a ballet slipper, and several locks of her hair. In the month of December, Elaine sent Elvis five to six letters, all containing locks of her hair. She wanted to make sure that Elvis received at least one of them for Christmas. Elaine's mother noticed the bald spots on her daughter's head and, in a panic, took her to the doctor. After four visits the perplexed doctor could find nothing physically wrong with Elaine. Finally, on their way back home after the fourth visit, Elaine, seeing her mother's great worry, told the truth about her hair. Her mother was furious. She yelled at her daughter for worrying her, for lying, and for doing such a stupid thing. She banned Elvis Presley from her daughter's life, taking away all her records, magazines, and photos, and reportedly had her seek help from a therapist!

One year, after giving a lot of thought to what to get his relatives and friends for Christmas, Elvis decided to do some window shopping. He needed some ideas and thought that by looking around a little, something might surface that he would like. In one store he spotted travel clocks handsomely set in rich leather casings. He loved how they looked and decided to buy them and give them out for Christmas.

On Christmas Eve in 1962, Elvis acted like the biggest child in the world as he celebrated the holiday at Graceland. He had the people closest to him around him, but could not wait to open his presents. During dinner he told his guests to hurry and after eating a seven course dinner in twenty minutes, Elvis gathered everyone in the living room for his gift-opening ceremony. He was as excited as a little boy. Elvis could never wait until Christmas morning to open his gifts as he was never able to contain his excitement and curiosity.

The gift giving ceremony at Graceland went like this: first, Elvis would open all of his gifts; next came the members of his entourage and their families; and then Elvis's staff. Vernon and Minnie Mae Presley went next, followed by Dee Stanley and her boys. The last person to receive and open gifts was Elvis's girlfriend or his wife.

Elvis began receiving Christmas gifts from his fans around September. By Christmas, there were so many cards, packages, and boxes that they had to be taken to the office behind Graceland. As the days passed, more gifts arrived. The office was so packed with gifts that no one could go inside. It would take Elvis and his secretaries two to three weeks to open all of these gifts!

Elvis's grandmother, Minnie Mae Presley, lost her wedding band sometime in the early winter of 1963. Although she had been divorced from her husband, Jessie D. Pressley, for many years, the band had become a part of her and she felt lost without it. Realizing that a new band would be the perfect gift for his grandmother, Elvis had his jeweler, Harry Levitsch, bring a selection of rings to Graceland so that he could choose the most appropriate one for her. Several days later, all of Memphis was buzzing with the news that Elvis was getting married!

Elvis gave out envelopes filled with money to his staff for Christmas in 1963. He did not want the responsibility of buying the wrong things and considered money the best gift. This way the recipients could spend the money the way they wanted to.

Elvis's entourage, known as the Memphis Mafia, presented Elvis with an elaborate leather-bound Bible as a Christmas gift in 1964. On one of the book's first pages was a drawing of a tree which was labeled "The Tree of Life." Each branch symbolized a member of the entourage and was inscribed with the man's name. Elvis was the trunk—the body which kept them all together. Elvis told many people that the Bible was one of the best gifts he had ever received from his men.

When Priscilla graduated from Immaculate Conception High School in 1963, Elvis bought her a red Corvair as a graduation gift. During the Christmas holidays in 1964, Elvis sold the car to Alan Fortas and his wife, Jo Tuneberg, for $1. The couple had just been married and they needed a vehicle. Priscilla was angry that Elvis had taken away her gift, but he promised he would buy her another one.

One Christmas in the mid-1960's, the Colonel decided to give gifts to the men of Elvis's entourage, which was something he had never done before. The men could not believe their eyes when they opened their packages and saw that

Parker had sent each of them a stuffed animal. Another year, the Colonel sent them his most prized possession: money! He sent the men $80—to be split seven ways.

In the mid-1960's, Elvis would get together with Joe Esposito, his right hand man, and have what he referred to as his, 'Christmas gift conference.' The men would discuss what type of gift to buy for whom.

The mid-1960's was a tumultuous time for Elvis and his entourage. Several times Elvis fired certain members of his staff only to rehire and refire them. As each man left, another came back. When the Christmas holidays came around, Elvis did not forget any of his men. To those working for him, Elvis gave out cash. To those fired, Elvis sent $100 money orders via special delivery.

One of Elvis's fans bought him a pet Spider monkey for Christmas in 1966. She wanted to give Elvis this gift on Christmas Day but because of his schedule she was forced to give it to him a few days after. She found out that Elvis was renting the Memphian Theater, located at 51 So. Cooper Street. She went down to the theater and waited inside for Elvis. During intermission, Elvis came out to the concession stand to get refreshments and she grabbed this opportunity to give him the monkey. Elvis got a big kick out of the gift and asked her how she came up with the idea. She told him that he had everything he could ever want or need and she wanted to give him something that he could get just pure pleasure out of. She also told him that she knew he liked animals and since the Spider monkey was small, it would be easy to care for.

After Dewey Phillips' death on September 28, 1968, his wife wrote Elvis a letter. In the letter she explained that she was in a very bad financial situation and was having a difficult time raising her two boys. For Christmas, Elvis wrote a check for $1,000 and had it delivered to Mrs. Phillips via special delivery. The money was a God-send in Mrs. Phillips' eyes as was Elvis. Without his help, the Phillips's would never have been able to survive.

For Christmas 1969, Vernon Presley and Dee Stanley decided to get Elvis a white silk robe. It was nearly impossible to find such a robe but Dee finally located one on Christmas Eve. When Elvis opened the gift the following day, he was delighted. The robe became his favorite piece of clothing.

On December 21, 1970, Elvis decided that he wanted to meet President Nixon at the White House. Elvis's bodyguard Sonny West accompanied him on the impromptu trip. On the flight from Memphis to Washington, D.C., Elvis struck up a conversation with a young soldier who had been in the war in Vietnam. The two discussed the Army for a while then talk turned to the Christmas holiday. When Elvis discovered that the soldier was returning home without any gifts he promptly took his money from Sonny and handed the entire $500 to the young man. The soldier, unsure of how to react to Elvis's unexpected display of generosity, saluted him. After the plane landed Sonny scolded Elvis for giving away all of their cash. Elvis solved the problem by having another member of his entourage fly out to D.C., with more.

Several days before Christmas in 1970, Elvis went to Robertson Motors located at 2950 Airways Boulevard and purchased several cars. For himself he bought a Mercedes Grand 600 for $25,000. He spent $9,000 for a Mercedes 280SEL and $7,700 each on two Mercedes 250s, all of which he gave away as Christmas gifts. A short time after Christmas that year, several popular fan magazines found out that Elvis had given away nine Mercedes for the holiday season. The magazines named him the "Big Giver of the Year" for 1970.

On Christmas Eve in 1970, Elvis and his father had a big fight. The argument erupted after Elvis spent $35,000 on guns for Christmas. Vernon knew that Elvis had purchased the firearms for his bodyguards and was angry. Vernon told his son that he was spending far more than was coming in and if he did not watch it, all the money would be gone. Elvis was angry. He did not like anyone getting involved in his financial affairs, especially his father, who was dependent on him after Vernon quit his job in the 1950's. Elvis angrily told his father that he had no right making any comments or suggestions as to how he spent his money. He told his father that he had better calm down or he would cut him off. Elvis was so furious that he threw a plate against the wall before storming to his room. Elvis stayed in his room, only coming down for dinner the following day, and he avoided his father.

In 1970, Elvis presented Bill Morris with a $9,000 4-door silver Mercedes 280 SEL. Morris, a former sheriff of Memphis, was mayor of the city at the time. Elvis picked Morris up at his house and took him for a drive before explaining that the car was a gift. Morris was thrilled. As he took his place behind the wheel and proceeded to drive back to his house, Elvis's "I'll Be Home for Christmas" played on the radio.

Elvis gave his Beverly Hills, California, chauffeur, Sir Gerald Peters, a gold Swiss watch for Christmas in 1970. Elvis truly liked Peters and wanted him to know so through this gift. Sir Gerald's real name was Gerald Saunderson and at one time he had served as chauffeur to Sir Winston Churchill, Prime Minister of England.

Three days before Christmas 1970, Elvis received a call from some of his old friends in Tupelo asking if he would come down to receive a special gift. Elvis was available on the 29th and promised to make the trip that day. He was a bit apprehensive, not knowing what to expect. When he arrived, he was presented a "Good Neighbor" plaque by Mr. and Mrs. Roy McComb and Mr. and Mrs. James Farrar. The plaque was engraved with "The Impossible Dream" and was given to him not because of who he was but because of how he had accomplished his dream. Elvis was touched by this gift and, in honor of it, promised to include the song "The Impossible Dream" on an upcoming album. His promise was kept when he sang this song at Madison Square Garden on June 10, 1972, and included it on his RCA album *Live in Madison Square Garden.*

Memphis sheriff Roy C. Nixon presented Elvis with a badge/belt buckle adorned with a sheriff's star for Christmas on December 31, 1970. Elvis was commissioned a special deputy by Nixon in a private ceremony. Mrs. Betty Malone gave Elvis the oath after he posted a $5,000 bond. Elvis later had diamonds added to the badge/belt buckle, which he wore when he served as best man at Sonny West's wedding on December 28, 1971.

Elvis went car crazy for Christmas in 1971, purchasing ten Mercedes from a dealership in Los Angeles for $85,000. After distributing the cars to his friends Elvis returned to Memphis where both Priscilla and Vernon scolded him for spending such an exorbitant amount of money. Angered by the reaction of both his wife and his father, Elvis decided to spend the rest of the Christmas holiday back in California.

On December 22, 1972 Elvis gave Colonel Parker a Christmas gift of a $1.2 million airplane. Never had an entertainer bestowed such an extravagant gift upon his manager, and the Colonel was ecstatic!

On December 25, 1972, Elvis spent his first Christmas without Priscilla. She had left him and all the divorce papers were filed and awaiting finalization. Elvis was in a very foul mood. With him was his new girlfriend, Linda Thompson, a beauty pageant winner and title holder of "Miss Tennessee." Trying to show everyone that he was not fazed by what Priscilla was doing, Elvis bought Linda a beautiful and very expensive mink coat for Christmas.

In 1972, Elvis sent his cousin Billy Smith to the local furrier with several thousand dollars and had him buy ten mink coats. In addition to the coat he had purchased for Linda Thompson, he also purchased coats for all of his bodyguards' wives or girlfriends for Christmas. The ladies were shocked upon receiving such gifts. When Priscilla found out she was furious that Elvis had spent so much money on these women and she made sure to scold him for it.

Several days before Christmas in 1972, Elvis asked Janelle McComb, one of his neighbors from Tupelo, to compose a poem for his daughter's fourth birthday. A few days later, McComb informed Elvis that the poem entitled, "The Priceless Gift," was complete. She traveled to Graceland to present him with a framed copy of the poem, which Elvis promptly took up to his bedroom to hide from Lisa Marie. When he came back downstairs, McComb noticed that he had been crying. She asked Elvis to sign her copy of the poem, and he wrote: "This is beautiful. Thank you, Elvis Presley." As he finished signing the copy, a lone tear landed on his signature. He tried to wipe the tear away, but only succeeded in smearing the autograph. He quickly apologized, but McComb interrupted, saying, "No! Someday that tear drop will be just as priceless as this poem is to you!"

For Christmas one year, Elvis presented all the men working on his shows and tours in Las Vegas with solid gold TCB charms complete with diamonds. Elvis came up with the "Taking Care of Business" logo and lightning bolt one day after talking about doing things fast—lightning fast. The women in the group received similar TLC charms, which stood for "Tender, Loving Care."

For Christmas, Linda Thompson bought Elvis a thick, heavy cross pendant made of gold and encrusted with small diamonds. In the center were two touching hearts. One was made of emeralds, Linda's birthstone, and the other was made of rubies, Elvis's birthstone. He loved it and wore it often on stage throughout the 1970's.

In the 1970's, when Elvis was in the mood to buy jewelry for Christmas, he contacted one of his jewelers, Lowell Hayes, and had him bring over a case full of expensive trinkets. After several years of buying his relatives and friends jewelry, Elvis had a hard time remembering what he had purchased for each individual. Not wanting to repeat an item, he had Hayes keep a list of what each person had. Elvis had a system for selecting the jewelry: he would first look through the case and, when something caught his eye, he would pick it up and examine it. Then he would think of the best person for that item. When he had someone matched with a piece of jewelry, Elvis would ask Hayes to check his list to make sure the person didn't have a similar piece and, if they did not, he would purchase it. After paying cash for the pieces Elvis would have Hayes take the jewelry back with him. Hayes would place each item in an envelope and write on it the name of the person who was to receive it. On Christmas Day, Hayes would drop by Graceland and give Elvis the envelopes, which were ready to distribute.

On December 15, 1973, the Las Vegas Hilton Hotel presented Elvis with a Christmas gift: a solid gold medallion with his name spelled out in diamonds. The medallion was valued at around $3,000. Elvis loved the fact that the hotel's owner, Barron Hilton, took good care of him and showed such appreciation for his business.

Several weeks before Christmas in 1974, Elvis was rummaging through the attic at Graceland when he stumbled across a box of never-opened copies of his first Christmas record *Elvis' Christmas Album* (LOC-1035). By that time the album was valued at $500, which made the box of 50 records worth $25,000! Elvis presented the albums to family, friends, and fans as Christmas gifts.

Colonel Parker received yet another new car for Christmas in 1974, a baby blue Cadillac. Parker drove the car back to his home in Madison, Tennessee, and showed the car to his wife, Marie. He proudly told her that "the boy" got it for him. One look at the car and Marie cringed. She exclaimed that she had never seen a more hideous color and she told her husband to take the car to the dealer and exchange it for another color. Parker, loving the car as it was, did not want to trade in his car nor did he want another model. The car Elvis had given him came fully equipped and he was not about to trade it for another one with less features just because Marie didn't like the color. He then got a grand idea: the next day he took the car into the body shop and had it painted white. This way he was happy with the model and Marie was happy with the new color.

Elvis and his cook, Mary Jenkins, were talking one day in December 1975. Mary had just finished making Elvis a sandwich and while he ate they chatted about life. During the conversation the subject came around to houses and cars. During that discussion, Elvis promised to buy Mary a house.

Several days before Christmas, Elvis and Mary went driving around Memphis and, when they reached 682 Devant Street, Mary showed Elvis her dream house. Elvis put Mary in the car and drove to the realtor's office. There, he asked the realtor and her assistant to bring the necessary paperwork to buy a house and to come with them. When they reached the house and the realtor opened the front door, Mary ran in and exclaimed that she loved it. Elvis immediately got out his checkbook and wrote a check for the full amount of the house! On their way back to the realty office, Elvis passed a car dealership. He made a U-turn and pulled into Sid Carroll's Pontiac at 1011 Union Avenue. He told Mary that since she had a new house for Christmas, she needed a new car to park out front. Mary was speechless. She and the other two ladies got out of the car and followed Elvis inside the showroom, where he selected for Mary a light blue 1975 Pontiac

Bonneville with a white vinyl top. Not to leave out the two ladies, Elvis also bought them brand new cars. Since the ladies now had their own cars, Elvis told them they could now drive back to where they needed to go, bade them goodbye, and wished them a Merry Christmas.

Charlie Hodge, who had been a friend of Elvis's since they met in the service in 1958, bought Elvis a beautiful fur coat as a Christmas present in 1975. Elvis was shocked by the gift because he knew Charlie did not have a lot of money. He suggested that Charlie keep the coat for himself, saying, "Since you liked the coat well enough to buy it for me, I'd like you to have it back!" Charlie was hurt at first, but he soon realized that Elvis was only acting in his best interest. He had always wanted a fur coat of his own, and now, thanks to Elvis's generosity, he had one.

Several days before Chrismtas in 1975, Elvis went down to the Southern Motors/Madison Cadillac showroom located at 341 Union Avenue at 3:00 in the morning. Elvis had called the manager an hour before and asked him to meet him. Elvis was in the mood to buy cars for his friends and ended up buying thirteen Cadillacs! The total amount he paid was $168,000, all spent in just one hour's time. Needless to say, there were may happy faces around Graceland on that Christmas morning.

In 1975, during Christmas week, the Sweet Inspirations ran through the Hilton Hotel lobby, screaming and flashing the rings that Elvis had given them for Christmas. The Sweet Inspirations, a popular vocal backup group, consisted of Emily (Cissy) Houston, Myrna Smith, Estelle Brown, and Sylvia Shemwell. They were Elvis's backup group for many years and also worked with other singers. They peformed with Aretha Franklin on her "Respect" recording.

In late fall of 1976, Vernon hired a painter to paint his portrait in rich oil colors. He wanted to give the painting to Elvis for Christmas. When the right painter was found, Vernon sat for him for an entire week. On Christmas Eve, Vernon presented Elvis with the large package. When Elvis opened it and saw the painting of his father, he had it positioned in the living room near the quarter wall separating the living room and the foyer, where it still hangs today.

On December 31, 1977, just after the first Christmas the world celebrated without Elvis, he was honored with a star on the Hollywood Walk of Fame. The star was placed at 6777 Hollywood Blvd., near Highland Avenue.

Elvis's January 6, 1957 appearance on The Ed Sullivan Show. *Elvis wears the gold lamé vest that Barbara Hearn gave to him for Christmas.*

Chief Wah-Nee-Ota helps Elvis put on the chief's bonnet, a gift from the Los Angeles Indian Tribal Council, in honor of his portrayal of a half-breed in Flaming Star. *Taken December 27, 1960, on the Twentieth Century Fox movie lot.*

Mingling with fans outside his 1174 Hillcrest Road home in Bel Air, California, mid-December 1968.

Elvis thanks his fans for the wonderful Christmas gifts. Bel Air, California, mid-December 1968.

Russell Stover Christmas candy, 1997.

Special promotional photo.

RCA Christmas postcard from 1967.

Elvis looks at a fancy wreath that one of his fans gave him for Christmas. Bel Air, California, mid-December 1968.

Elvis stands near the gold wreath which was presented to him in Bel Air, California, mid-December 1968.

Russell Stover ad for 5 new Christmas candy sets, 1998.

Elvis holds his Christmas gift as he hugs Sue Kuna in Bel Air, California, on December 5, 1968.

Bel Air, California, December 5, 1968.

During the Christmas holidays in 1968, Elvis met with fans outside his Hillcrest Rd. home in Bel Air, California.

Special brochure and mail offer for an Elvis portrait for special Christmas gifts (1979).

Elvis gets snapped by a fan as he walks up to mingle at the gates of his 1174 Hillcrest Road home in mid-December 1968.

A lucky fan is granted her Christmas wish: to meet Elvis. (Mid-December, 1968.)

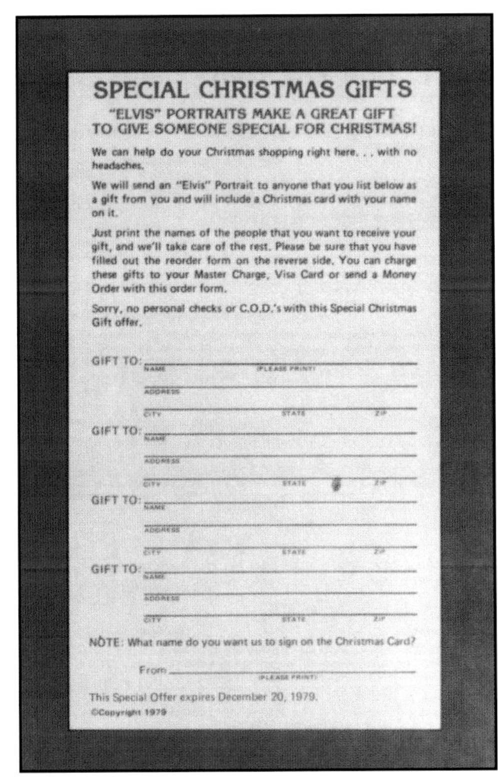

SPECIAL CHRISTMAS GIFTS

"ELVIS" PORTRAITS MAKE A GREAT GIFT
TO GIVE SOMEONE SPECIAL FOR CHRISTMAS!

We can help do your Christmas shopping right here. . . with no headaches.

We will send an "Elvis" Portrait to anyone that you list below as a gift from you and will include a Christmas card with your name on it.

Just print the names of the people that you want to receive your gift, and we'll take care of the rest. Please be sure that you have filled out the reorder form on the reverse side. You can charge these gifts to your Master Charge, Visa Card or send a Money Order with this order form.

Sorry, no personal checks or C.O.D.'s with this Special Christmas Gift offer.

GIFT TO: ______________________
NAME (PLEASE PRINT)
ADDRESS
CITY STATE ZIP

GIFT TO: ______________________
NAME
ADDRESS
CITY STATE ZIP

GIFT TO: ______________________
NAME
ADDRESS
CITY STATE ZIP

GIFT TO: ______________________
NAME
ADDRESS
CITY STATE ZIP

NOTE: What name do you want us to sign on the Christmas Card?

From ______________________
(PLEASE PRINT)

This Special Offer expires December 20, 1979.
©Copyright 1979

Mail-in section of the "Portraits of the Stars." Expiration date 12-20-1979.

Elvis leaving his Bel Air, California, home in his Cadillac, mid-December 1968.

Elvis at his front gates in Bel Air, California, mid-December 1968.

The painting of Vernon which he gave to Elvis for Christmas. Front of card #175 of the Elvis Collection by the River Group, 1992.

Having just received a Santa Claus from one of his fans, Elvis drives back into his Bel Air, California, home on December 5, 1970.

175

This stunning portrait of Vernon Elvis Presley hangs in the living room at Graceland. The painting was a gift that Vernon presented to Elvis during Christmas 1976 — the last Christmas they spent together. Elvis died the next summer; Vernon passed away on June 26, 1979 — two years to the day after Elvis' last concert performance. Today, the painting is a tribute to the love between father and son.

THE Elvis COLLECTION

Elvis, Elvis Presley and The Elvis Collection are Registered Trademarks of Elvis Presley Enterprises, Inc. Copyright 1992 © 1992 The River Group, Printed in U.S.A.

Back of card #175 of the Elvis Collection by the River Group, 1992.

Pop-up card from Pop Shots.

Double-sided Elvis Christmas gift bag, comes in two colors. Green side shown here. From American Greetings, 1995.

Chapter 10
A Charitable Christmas

Elvis participated in a charity Christmas show at the Memphis Ellis Auditorium on December 15, 1955. Also on the bill were Slim Rhodes and his Mountaineers and teen tap dancer Jo Haynes. Elvis performed in a wrestling ring, as famous wrestlers Al "Spider" Galento, Gorgeous George, and Sputnik Monroe had hosted their annual benefit show the night before and there wasn't enough time to clear the auditorium. Money raised from this performance benefited the Memphis Press Scimitar's Goodfellows Organization and the *Memphis Commercial Appeal*'s Basket Fund.

In November 1956, Elvis was the first person to purchase Christmas Seals in Southern Nevada. Roxanne Crosley and Marilyn Evans, chorus girls from the New Frontier Hotel, also bought seals at that same time. The transactions, handled by publicity chairman Scott Griffith, were made public through photographs in the newspapers.

Beginning in 1956, Elvis hand-delivered his Christmas charity donations to Mayor Ingram's office in downtown Memphis. Members of the press were always on hand for the event. Elvis enjoyed posing for photographs with all fifty envelopes fanned out in front of him, each containing a check for $1,000 for Memphis charities.

In 1958, while in the Army stationed in Germany, Elvis made a donation of $1,500 to the Landesjugendenheim Steinmuehle Orphanage. Approximately 115 children lived at the orphanage at the time, which was located in Obererlenbach near where Elvis was stationed in Friedberg. Elvis understood the pain of the orphaned children, having recently lost his mother, and he wanted to ensure that Christmas was a happy time for them.

Vernon Presley visited the *Memphis Press-Scimitar* newspaper's city room on Christmas Eve in 1961 as a personal messenger from Santa Claus. He presented Mrs. Jean Hardendorf, the newspaper's librarian, with a $1,000 check from his son to be donated to the paper's Goodfellows Organization. The money helped to ensure that four thousand underprivileged children would be given clothes and toys and that they would enjoy both Christmas and New Year's Eve parties. Elvis donated $1,000 to the organization each year until his death in 1977.

In the early 1960's, Elvis donated $900 to the R.O.T.C. of his alma mater, L.C. Humes High School. The money went towards the purchase of new uniforms for the annual "Spirit of Christmas" parade. When Elvis was a student at L.C. Humes, he was a member of the U.S. Military high school training program.

A few days before Christmas in 1963, Elvis and his father visited the Memphis Courthouse to distribute $1,000 checks to local charities. Elvis wore a black suit with a double-breasted top coat with a velvet collar for the occasion. When the charities presented Elvis with a six-foot high walnut plaque in honor of his donations, he joked that he would have to build a special room to accommodate the large plaque. Everyone laughed and applauded the "King of Hearts." The plaque remains on display at the Graceland mansion in the Hall of Gold.

On Christmas Eve 1963, Elvis jumped into his new Rolls Royce and drove around Memphis, making stops at all the charities. He parked his exotic and very expensive car and ran inside to present his annual Christmas donation. Elvis created quite a scene that day as he hand delivered his donations.

Sometime in 1963, Elvis met a young nun from the Convent of the Good Shepherd in Memphis. He took a liking to her and her shy demeanor and he sent her a check as his Christmas donation to her order. Elvis had the check hand-delivered by one of his men and on the envelope he wrote, "God Bless You! Love, Elvis." The young nun was speechless and very grateful.

Elvis gave Los Angeles Police Chief Ed M. Davis a Christmas donation for the International Association of Chiefs of Police in the 1960's. The money was used to purchase toys for poor children and to obtain new uniforms for the LAPD marching band. On December 3, 1970, Elvis donated another $7,000 to the Los Angeles Police Department. Again the money was used to purchase toys and to buy new uniforms.

Shortly before Christmas sometime in the mid 1960's, Elvis purchased dozens of $1 tickets for a raffle benefiting the local Little League baseball team. The first prize was an ornate, silver-covered saddle valued at $10,000. Elvis was pleasantly surprised to be contacted by the organization and informed that he'd been selected as the first prize winner. Although he usually turned down prizes so that the sponsoring organization could benefit, Elvis was so taken with this saddle that he accepted the prize. The saddle remains at Graceland today.

Several days before Christmas in 1965, Elvis promised Memphis Mayor Henry Loeb that he would attend a party being held on Christmas Eve for the benefit of local charities. Unfortunately, the media found out about Elvis's plan and, not wishing to create a mob scene, Elvis was forced to cancel his appearance. The Colonel called the Mayor and offered his apologies on behalf of Elvis, telling Loeb that Elvis had a previous engagement. Vernon attended the party in his son's place and presented Elvis's annual donations to the charities.

In 1966, Elvis distributed checks to Memphis charities. There were thirty-nine charities that Elvis helped that year. His usual donation amount was $1,000 and was always delivered on Christmas Day. Two of the charities Elvis always helped out were The American Legion Christmas Basket Fund and the *Memphis Press-Scimitar*'s, Goodfellow Christmas Fund.

Elvis promotion by the American Cancer Society, 1956/1957. Card #629 of the Elvis Collection by the River Group.

Elvis lifting March of Dimes girl Mary Kosloski, at Graceland in 1957. Mary thanked Elvis for his Christmas donation.

Memphis, October 1957. Promotion for high school championship football game held on Thanksgiving Day. Proceeds from the game were given to the Foundation for the Blind. Elvis donated $15,000.

18 kt. gold plated Elvis Christmas ornament. American Greetings, 1995.

Rare version of the 1963 bonus photo calendar from the Girls! Girls! Girls! *soundtrack album.*

Elvis takes time out from the filming of It Happened at the World's Fair *to sign Christmas donation checks for Memphis charities. Vernon Presley and Memphis mayor Mark King are on hand as Elvis signs the fifty $1,000 checks on November 8, 1962, in Hollywood, California.*

Christmas morning, 1962. Vernon Presley hand delivers Elvis's Christmas donations to Memphis charities. Gathered in front of City Hall, charity representatives wave Elvis's checks and his 1963 calendar.

Elvis in Mayor Ingram's office in Memphis, fanning fifty envelopes, each containing a $1,000 Christmas charity donation. December 18, 1963.

Fan photo greeting card.

Fan photo greeting card.

Plaque listing the fifty charities to which Elvis gave annual Christmas donations.

Fan photo greeting card.

Fan club Christmas greeting card.

Holiday edition of a cookbook benfitting The Elvis Presley Memorial Trauma Center in Memphis. All recipes supplied by Elvis's family, friends, and fans.

On the set of Trouble with Girls, *Elvis receives the Guide Dog for the Blind Award from Great Britain fan club. (1969)*

Elvis receives the Kui-Lee Cancer Fund Award for his tremendous benefit show at the Honolulu International Arena on January 14, 1973.

Double-sided Elvis Christmas gift bag, American Greetings, 1995.
Red side shown here.

Christmas ornament, 1990's by Topperscot, Inc.

Chapter 11
Christmas in Memphis

On Christmas Eve in 1970, Elvis met jeweler Lowell Hayes at the Memphian Movie Theater. During intermission of the movie, Elvis and Lowell went into the men's restroom to look at the items the jeweler had brought with him. Lowell continued to supply Elvis with countless pieces of jewelry for Christmas for years to come.

Elvis's bodyguard, Sonny West, married Judy Morgan on December 28, 1970, in a Christmas-themed wedding at the Trinity Baptist Church in Memphis. Elvis served as best man and Priscilla was the maid of honor. As his wedding present, Elvis paid for the Wests' wedding and gave them a car along with a sizeable check.

While in Tupelo, Mississippi, on December 29, 1970, Elvis visited his old school chum, Guy Harris, who was a sergeant with the local police department. He also saw Bill Mitchell, the Lee County Sheriff at the County Jail. Elvis was happy to see his old friends and to be able to spend time with them during the Christmas season.

During the 1970's, Elvis made it a rule never to talk about any of the Christmas presents he bought for his relatives and friends. He did not want anyone to disclose the information about what each person was going to receive. Elvis loved surprising people. He thought that Christmas Eve was the day to open the gifts and no one should know what they were to receive until then. One of the rules he set was that there was to be no talking about Christmas presents around Graceland.

On Christmas Eve in 1972, Elvis stormed out of a screening at the Memphian Movie Theater. Despite efforts of his girlfriend, Linda Thompson, Elvis remained in a rotten mood. He was distraught over the loss of his wife, who had recently left him for another man. When they got to Graceland, Elvis walked upstairs to his room and slammed the door.

Although it was a Graceland tradition to open gifts on Christmas Eve, Elvis did not come downstairs that year. It if hadn't been for Lisa Marie, Elvis might never have come down on Christmas Day. As it was, he watched his daughter open her gifts but left his untouched under the tree.

Around the Christmas holiday in 1973, Elvis wasn't feeling well and was admitted to the Baptist Memorial Hospital for some tests. A nurse named Clara Lee Mayhew made sure that he was comfortable, dispensed his medicine, and kept an eye on her famous patient. The day before Elvis was to undergo the tests, Nurse Mayhew discovered that he was missing. While frantically searching the hospital, she was passing the children's ward when she heard his beautiful voice. She went into the room and was welcomed to a most beautiful sight: Elvis dressed in a thick white robe, his jet black hair perfectly coifed, sitting amongst wide-eyed cherubs, singing "Blue Christmas." Elvis was saddened by the fact that most of these children would have to spend Christmas in the hospital. In addition to his Christmas serenade, Elvis also had presents brought to all the sick children.

When Elvis did his Christmas shopping he was always under stress. He could not walk around without hundreds of people surrounding him. He loved to Christmas shop and finally thought of the perfect solution: he asked the managers of his favorite stores if they could either stay open after hours or open their store especially for him. Every store agreed to do as he wished. Clerks, assistants, and tailors were kept on hand for Elvis's personal use. Elvis was now able to buy anything he wanted without fan interference. The store owners and managers were only too happy to oblige because they knew Elvis would spend more than enough to compensate for the extra expense.

In 1974, it seemed the entire world was having an energy crisis. Governments were asking people to conserve as much energy as possible. Elvis abided by all the rules and helped out whenever he could. During this energy crisis, Elvis did not '"light up" Graceland for Christmas as he had done in prior years.

When Elvis first got his plane, the "Lisa Marie," in November 1975, he had it customized and repainted and by the time Christmas arrived it was finished. After dinner on Christmas Day, Elvis told his friends and family members to put on their coats. He then packed them into several cars and drove them to the Memphis airport to see his plane. Elvis lead everyone through the terminal and showed them the Convair 880 from the window. Everyone told Elvis that the plane was beautiful. It was painted white with blue and gold accents and sported his famous TCB logo on the tail. Elvis then surprised his party with the news that he was flying all of them to Nashville.

Close to midnight on Christmas Day, Elvis's plane landed in Nashville. Elvis's pilot, Captain Elwood David, was a superb pilot and landed the plane without a bump. Elvis then asked his friends and family members what they thought about the flight and, when he got the remarks he wanted to hear, Elvis had Captain David fly them all back to Memphis.

Elvis decided to visit the local Memphis police station on Christmas Day in 1975. When he walked inside the station, the duty officer was shocked to see him and asked Elvis why he was there. Elvis joked that it was the only place open on Christmas Day. He then laughed and said that he was actually there to wish them a Merry Christmas and to thank them for doing such a great job around Memphis. He also thanked them for all the special work they did for him. The officers, now all gathered in the station lobby, told him that they enjoyed doing anything they could for him. Elvis was touched.

During the Christmas holidays in 1976, Elvis met a young couple who had just gotten married. To celebrate the happy occasion, Elvis offered to but them a car. The couple said that they liked the new Pontiac Grand Prix. They found a light blue model at Sid Carroll's Pontiac, located at 1011 Union Avenue in Memphis. Elvis immediately put a call in to the manager at his home. When the man realized it was 1:30 in the morning he refused to open the showroom. He told Elvis to come back in the morning when the showroom was open for business and hung up the phone.

Furious at how he was being treated after he had purchased dozens of cars from them, Elvis cursed out loud. Elvis then took the couple down the street to Schilling-Lincoln Mercury at 987 Union Avenue where the manager was more than willing to accommodate Elvis. A happy Elvis told the couple to look around and choose the car they liked. Ten minutes later the couple exclaimed that they were only interested in the Grand Prix. When Elvis explained that Lincolns were by far better cars and that he would not do business with Sid Carroll's, the couple grew adamant. They finally left the showroom, leaving an angry and flabbergasted Elvis standing alone with the manager.

Elvis sitting atop his horse, Rising Sun, at Graceland in December 1969.

Elvis at Graceland in December 1969, sitting atop his horse, Rising Sun, and mingling with fans.

One of Elvis's favorite photos. Taken at Graceland on December 25, 1970. Elvis and his friends hold up their newly-acquired badges from Sheriff Roy Nixon. Back row, left to right: Billy Smith, Lamar Fike, Jerry Schilling, Sheriff Roy Nixon, Vernon Presley, Sonny West, Charlie Hodge, George Klein, and Marty Lacker. Front row, left to right: Dr. Nick, Elvis, and Red West.

Elvis with Sheriff Roy Nixon at Graceland, Christmas 1970.

Elvis and Sonny West fix each other's ties moments before Sonny's wedding to Judy Morgan on December 28, 1970, at the Trinty Baptist Church in Memphis, Tennessee.

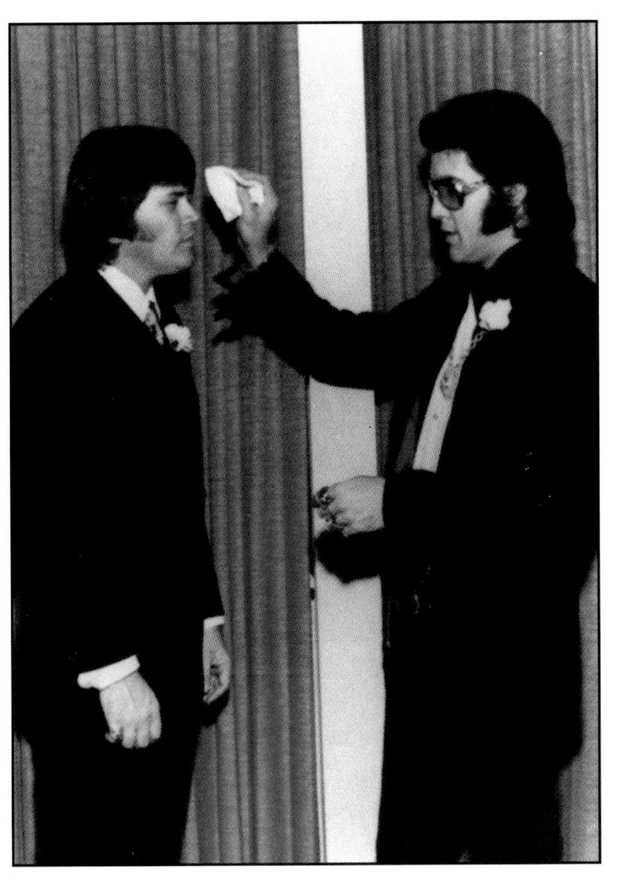

Elvis wiping the sweat off of Sonny West's brow minutes before Sonny's wedding, December 28, 1970.

December 28, 1970. Elvis serves as best man for Sonny West at his wedding to Judy Morgan at the Trinity Baptist Church in Memphis.

Elvis driving his new Stutz Blackhawk car in Bel Air, California, on December 5, 1970.

Christmas greeting card Ralph Wolfe Cowen, 1980's.

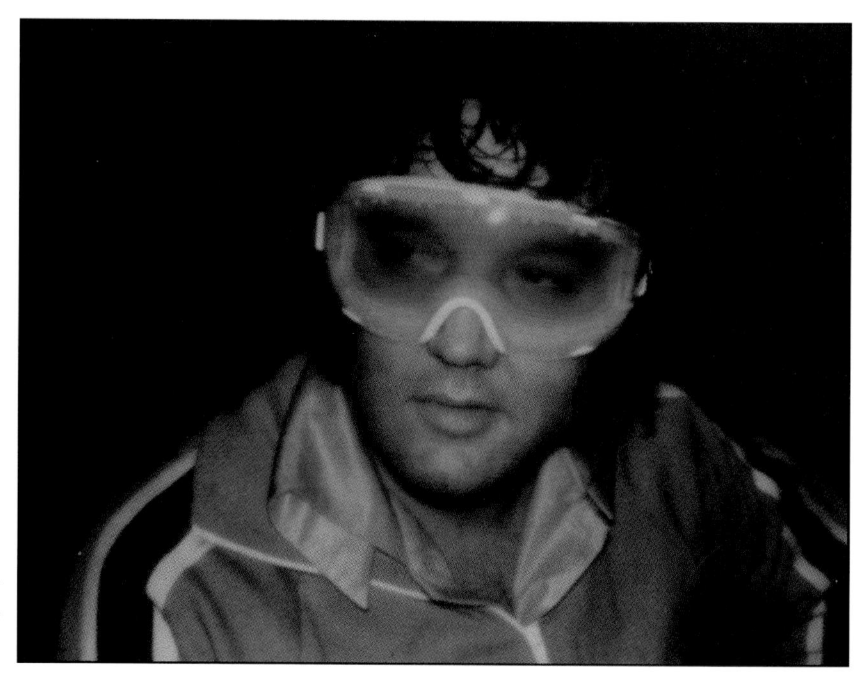

Elvis wears his protective eye wear as he snowmobiles during Christmas in 1976.

Fan club Christmas greeting card.

Rare RCA record streamer posted in record stores to promote Elvis's "Blue Christmas" 45rpm single, November 1964.

Chapter 12
The Christmas Sessions

Steve Sholes from RCA-Victor was the person who arranged and organized Elvis's first Christmas album. He talked with Elvis about it on September 2 or 3, 1957, after Elvis finished his two shows at the Rainier Ballpark in Seattle, Washington. When Elvis heard that he was to do a Christmas album he told Steve that he had always wanted to record Christmas music because it was his favorite time of year.

Elvis cut only two songs during his first day at Radio Recorders on September 5, 1957. RCA executives were furious that they had spent an entire day and gotten only two songs. To keep Elvis out of trouble, Steve Sholes and engineer Thorne Nogar blamed the band for the poor output.

RCA was short one song for the Christmas album, so executives asked the famous songwriting duo of Leiber and Stoller to compose a bluesy tune for Elvis. The result, "Santa Claus is Back in Town," turned out to be one of Elvis's best Christmas songs.

The real reason why Elvis decided to record a Christmas album in 1957 was to earn the respect, approval, and acceptance of his fans' parents. He did not want to be hated and blamed for all the wrong-doings and wanted the older generation to see that he was just a singer. He figured that everyone listened to Christmas music, and that is was the best way to have them think again about him and his music.

Scotty Moore, Bill Black, and DJ Fontana wanted to record an album, which they discussed with Colonel Parker and Tom Diskin, the Colonel's right hand man. The men, who composed Elvis's band, The Blue Moon Boys, had backed Elvis since 1954 and, by 1957, they were in desperate need of money. They were held on a retainer of $100 a week for every week they stayed home and $200 a week for every week they were on tour. Slowly but surely, as Elvis's fame increased, the boys were being cut out of his career. The retainer kept them exclusive to Elvis so they could not get other jobs to support their families. To keep the boys quiet, Parker promised them things that would never happen. On the last day of Elvis's Christmas sessions at Radio Recorders, Scotty, Bill, and DJ were promised studio time so that they could start laying down some instrumental tracks for their upcoming album. The minute they started playing, Tom Diskin walked in and told them that there had been some kind of mistake because the studio had booked someone else in that slot. They had to pack up their gear and leave. The men were devastated. Parker promised them another studio date in the near future, but that day never came.

In order to have an album ready for Christmas release, Elvis had to record sometime in May or June. To help with the holiday spirit, the Colonel had Alan Fortas dress up as Santa Claus and parade around the studio.

Elvis went into the studio to record "If Everyday Was Like Christmas" on June 10, 1966. He was having trouble getting into a Christmas mood and some of the RCA people began to panic. Several calls were made and suddenly the studio was transformed into a winter wonderland, complete with a Christmas tree and red lights. The air conditioner was even turned up to simulate cold weather. Elvis loved the change. He attempted the song once again, and this time the recording was perfect. He also cut "I'll Remember You" and "Indescribably Blue" that day, two songs which are considered among his best.

Recording sessions for *Elvis Sings the Wonderful World of Christmas* were held in Studio B at the RCA Nashville studios, May 15-21, 1971. The sessions were held in three sections: 6-9 p.m., 9:15 p.m.-12 a.m., and 1-4 a.m. After each song was cut, Elvis would go around the room and ask people their opinions of the take. Everyone offered him lavish compliments, except his karate instructor, a Chinese man by the name of Kang Rhee. In his heavy accent, he replied, "Oh, not so good!" For the duration of the sessions, Elvis consulted with the instructor and a take was selected only after it met with Kang Rhee's approval.

On May 15, 1971, Elvis recorded the song, "I'll Be Home on Christmas Day." He also re-recorded it in June 1971. RCA now had two different versions and had to decide which one to release. After playing both songs several times, RCA chose the version Elvis did in May. They said that the second version did not have as happy a feeling as the first.

On May 15, 1971, Elvis recorded "It Won't Seem Like Christmas Without You," "If I Get Home on Christmas Day," "Holly Leaves and Christmas Trees," "Merry Christmas Baby," "Silver Bells," "I'll Be Home on Christmas Day," "On a Snowy Christmas Night," "Winter Wonderland," "O Come, All Ye Faithful," "The First Noel," and "The Wonderful World of Christmas."

Elvis had a hard time reading the lyrics while recording "It Won't Seem Like Christmas Without You." The print was too small and he was getting quite aggravated. In addition, Elvis was having a problem with his throat. Several takes of the song were ruined because the microphone picked up the sound of Elvis clearing his throat.

For the recording of the *Elvis Sings the Wonderful World of Christmas* album, Elvis was having an extremely difficult time with the mood and ambiance. It was May and the weather was warm. There was nothing to make Elvis feel the Christmas spirit. The RCA staff sent some people to get decorations and an artificial Christmas tree to set up in the studio. Elvis walked in just as the staff was finishing up. He was in a foul mood and felt that RCA was playing with his head and trying to force him to record. They had done this before, but Elvis was in no mood this day. He went over to the Christmas tree and karate-kicked it. It fell backwards and crashed to the floor, causing most of the ornaments to shatter. The session was a disaster. Elvis did not sing or record one song well, and halfway through the day, the RCA executives told Elvis to go home, which he did.

Elvis was not pleased with *Elvis Sings the Wonderful World of Christmas* because of its lack of decent songs. He was to sing old traditional songs such as "Silver Bells," and "Winter Wonderland," when he really wanted new material that no one else had recorded. He wanted to be known as an original rather than a cover artist.

On December 10, 1973, Elvis recorded "It's Midnight" at the Stax Recording Studio in Memphis. It was quite a shock to see Elvis in a recording studio during the Christmas season. It was the first and last time he ever went into a recording studio on his own.

Gold foil sticker that was on the original seal of Elvis' Christmas Album.

Elvis at Radio Recorders in Hollywood, California, on September 5, 1957, for a recording session that resulted in his first Christmas album, Elvis' Christmas Album.

Rare 1957 music sheet of "Blue Christmas," one of Elvis's most famous Christmas songs.

1968 jukebox record strip of the reissue record.

Rare music sheet from 1957.

French Jukebox magazine (June/July/August 1985), featuring Elvis' Christmas Album *from England on the cover.*

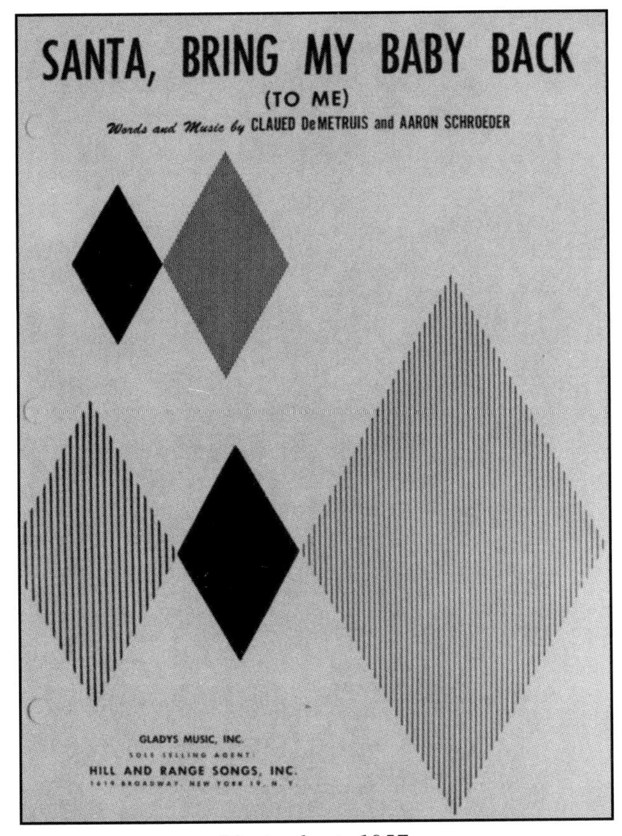

Music sheet, 1957.

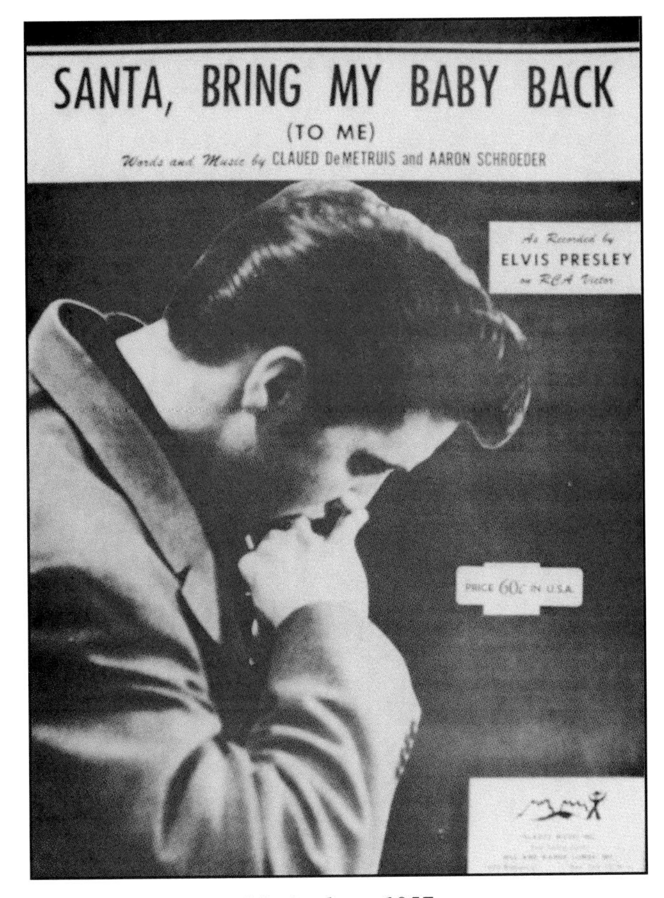

Music sheet, 1957.

Music sheet from London, England, 1964.

Billboard BEST BETS FOR CHRISTMAS

While dealers report that it is early for Christmas product, certain LP's and singles seem to be jumping out in front of others. It appears that Christmas LP's do not require the radio exposure as do the singles, and LP sales seem to be slightly ahead of singles sales to date. Below is a list of the best selling LP's and singles to date. As the sales of Christmas product increase, so too will the number of best selling Christmas LP's and singles reported in these special charts—in accordance with sound research practices in terms of sufficient retailers reporting significant sales on specific records. These special charts will run for the next five issues as a special buying and stocking guide. NOTE: It is possible that many new Christmas releases have not yet had the full opportunity to be reflected here.

CHRISTMAS LP'S 1966

1. MERRY CHRISTMAS—Andy Williams, Columbia CL 2420 (M); CS 9220 (S)
2. ELVIS' CHRISTMAS ALBUM—Elvis Presley, RCA Victor LPM 1951 (M); LSP 1951 (S)
3. THE DEAN MARTIN CHRISTMAS ALBUM—Reprise R 6222 (M); RS 6222 (S)
4. THE LITTLE DRUMMER BOY—Harry Simeone Chorale, 20th Century-Fox TFM 3100 (M); TFS 4100 (S)
5. MERRY CHRISTMAS—Bing Crosby, Decca DL 8128 (M); DL 78128 (S)
6. NOEL—Joan Baez, Vanguard VRS 9230 (M); VSD 79230 (S)
7. MERRY CHRISTMAS—Johnny Mathis, Columbia CL 1195 (M); CS 8021 (S)
8. THE CHRISTMAS SONG—Nat King Cole, Capitol W 1967 (M); SW 1967 (S)
9. O BAMBINO/THE LITTLE DRUMMER BOY—Harry Simeone Chorale, Kapp KL 1450 (M); KS 3450 (S)
10. SONGS FOR A MERRY CHRISTMAS—Wayne Newton, Capitol T 2588 (M); ST 2588 (S)
11. NAVIDAD MEANS CHRISTMAS—Eydie Gorme & Trio Los Panchos, Columbia CL 2557 (M); CS 9357 (S)
12. SEASONS GREETINGS FROM PERRY COMO—RCA Victor LPM 2066 (M); LSP 2066 (S)
13. THE SOUND OF CHRISTMAS—Ramsey Lewis Trio, Cadet CLP 687 (M); CLPS 687 (S)
14. SONGS FOR CHRISTMAS—Mahalia Jackson, Columbia CL 1903 (M); CS 8703 (S)
15. JAMES BROWN SINGS CHRISTMAS SONGS—King 1010 (M); (No Stereo)
16. MERRY CHRISTMAS—Supremes, Motown 638 (M); ST 638 (S)
17. HOLIDAY CHEER—Dean Martin, Capitol T 2343 (M); ST 2343 (S)
18. JOHN GARY CHRISTMAS ALBUM—RCA Victor LPM 2940 (M); LSP 2940 (S)
19. JACK JONES CHRISTMAS ALBUM—Kapp KL 1399 (M); KS 3399 (S)
20. MERRY CHRISTMAS—Brenda Lee, Decca DL 4583 (M); DL 74583 (S)
21. CHRISTMAS WONDERLAND—Bert Kaempfert & His Ork, Decca DL 4441 (M); DL 74441 (S)
22. HOLIDAY SING-ALONG WITH MITCH—Mitch Miller & the Gang, Columbia CL 1701 (M); CS 8501 (S)
23. HERE WE COME A-CAROLING—Ray Conniff & the Singers, Columbia CL 2408 (M); CS 9206 (S)
24. CHRISTMAS TIME—Roger Williams, Kapp KL 1164 (M); KS 3048 (S)
25. MORE SOUNDS OF CHRISTMAS—Ramsey Lewis Trio, Cadet CLP 745 (M); CLPS 745 (S)
26. A MERRY MANCINI CHRISTMAS—Henry Mancini Ork & Chorus, RCA Victor LPM 3612 (M); LSP 3612 (S)
27. CHRISTMAS WITH BUCK OWENS—Capitol T 2396 (M); ST 2396 (S)
28. CHRISTMAS WITH CHET ATKINS—RCA Victor LPM 2423 (M); LSP 2423 (S)
29. CHRISTMAS CAROLS OF EUROPE—Prague Madrigal Singers, Crossroads 22160053 (M); 22160054 (S)

CHRISTMAS SINGLES

1. THE LITTLE DRUMMER BOY—Harry Simeone Chorale, 20th Century-Fox 429
2. IF EVERY DAY WAS LIKE CHRISTMAS—Elvis Presley, RCA Victor 8950
3. PLEASE COME HOME FOR CHRISTMAS—Charles Brown, King 5405
4. SLEEP IN HEAVENLY PEACE (Silent Night)—Barbra Streisand, Columbia 43896
5. JINGLE BELL ROCK—Bobby Helms, Decca 30513
6. LONESOME CHRISTMAS—Lowell Fulson, Hollywood 1022
7. THE CHRISTMAS SONG—Nat King Cole, Capitol 3561
8. WHITE CHRISTMAS—Bing Crosby, Decca 23778
9. BAREFOOT SANTA CLAUS—Sonny James, Capitol 5733
10. SWEET LITTLE BABY BOY—James Brown & His Famous Flames, King 6065
11. ALL I WANT FOR CHRISTMAS IS YOU—Carla Thomas, Stax 206
12. BLUE CHRISTMAS—Elvis Presley, RCA Victor 0647
13. SILENT NIGHT—Bing Crosby, Decca 23777
14. ROCKIN' AROUND THE CHRISTMAS TREE—Brenda Lee, Decca 30776
15. SILVER BELLS—Al Martino, Capitol 5311
16. LITTLE DRUMMER BOY—Joan Baez, Vanguard 35046
17. WHITE CHRISTMAS—Drifters, Atlantic 1048

Billboard song chart, "Best Bets for Christmas," 1966.
LPs List: #2 is Elvis' Christmas Album.
Singles List: # 2 is "If Everyday was Like Christmas."

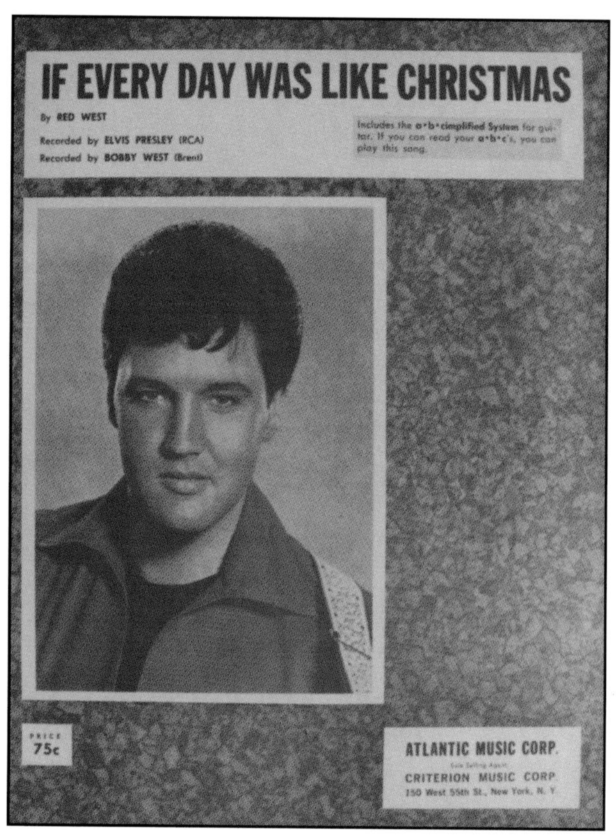

Music sheet, 1966.

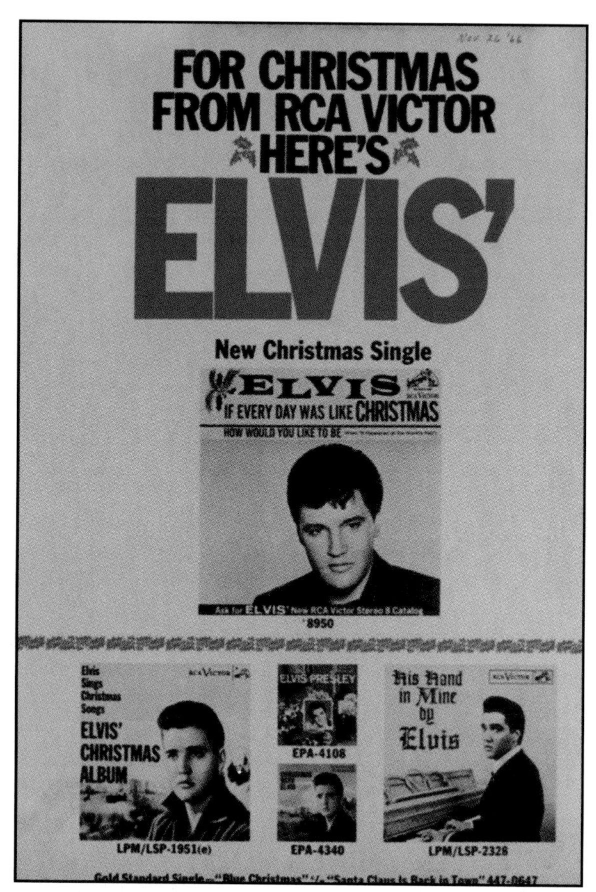

RCA full page record ad in Billboard *magazine dated November 26, 1966.*

Elvis receives an RIAA gold record for his first Christmas album, Elvis' Christmas Album, *while on the set of* Tickle Me.

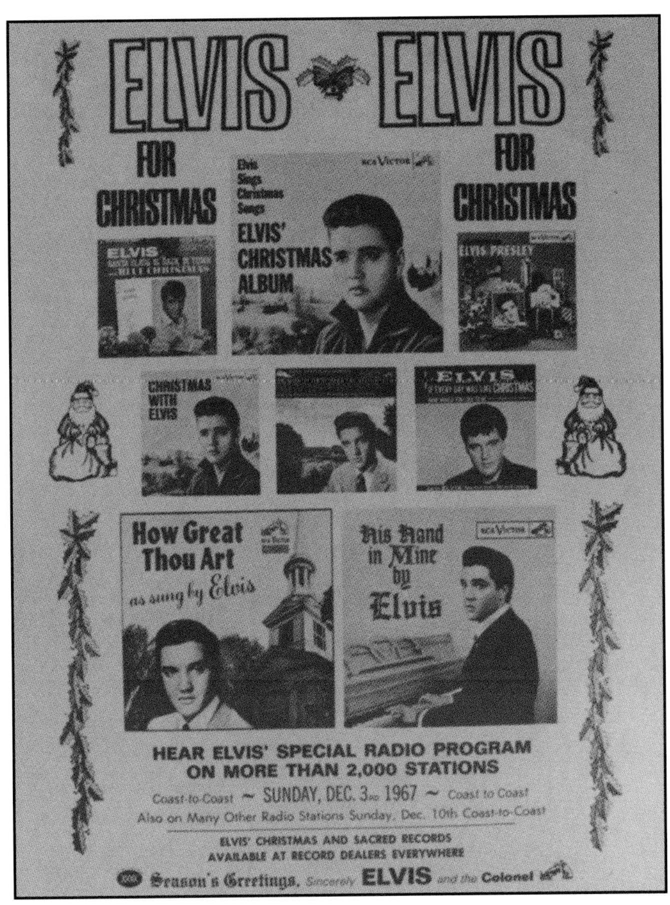

Flyers handed out to customers by record stores to promote Elvis' Christmas releases, 1966.

RCA Christmas program catalog lists all 2,000 radio stations which would air the special on December 3 and December 10, 1967. Also contains greetings from Elvis, the Colonel, and their various companies.

Cover of box containing the 7 1/2 reel-to-reel audio tape for radio stations to air on December 3 and December 10, 1967. Only 3,000 were made.

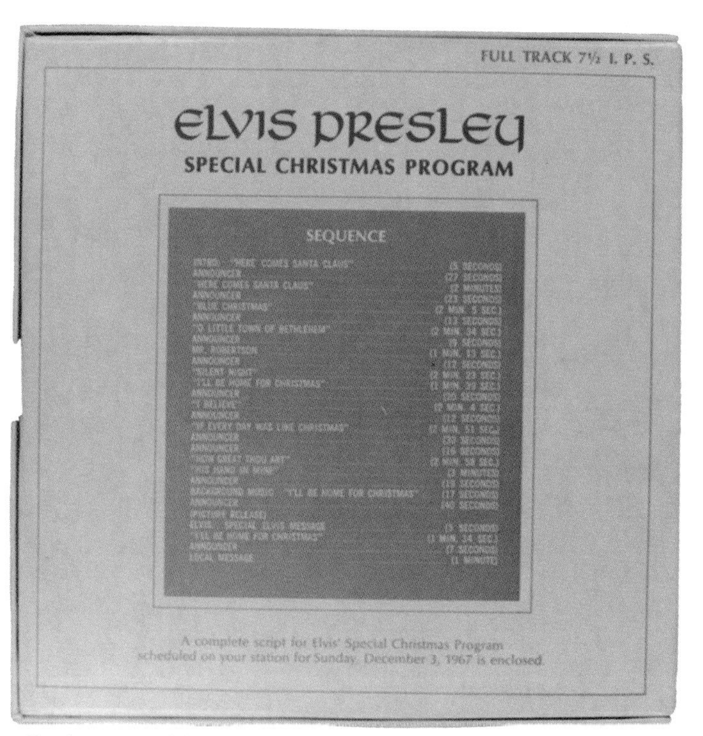

Back cover of the box containing the 7 1/2 reel-to-reel audio tape, made exclusively for radio stations.

Inside contents of the 7 1/2 reel-to-reel audio tape box. Includes the reel as well as a four page brochure containing dialogue for the disc jockey. (1967)

RCA cardboard record display for Elvis's Camden release, 1970.

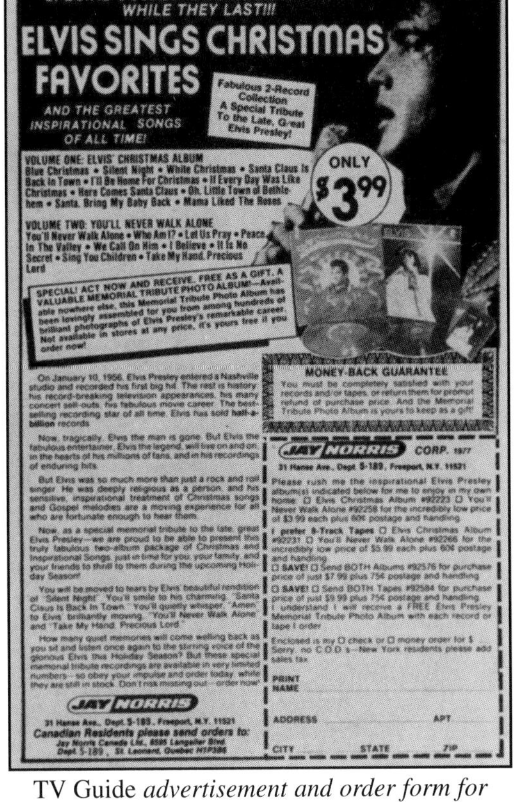

TV Guide *advertisement and order form for* Elvis' Christmas Album *and* You'll Never Walk Alone *LP from the Jay Morris Company, October 15, 1977.*

RCA jukebox strips, 1971.

Songbook by the Big 3 Music Corp., 1971. Contains music and lyrics to eighteen of Elvis's songs as well as other well known Christmas songs. (#83-3233)

Dear D.J. Please play

By: Elvis Presley.
This is on his Christmas Album(or a single)
titled:

This is on the RCA-Victor label.Thanks,

Merry Christmas !

Promo card sent to disc jockeys to encourage them to play Elvis's "Oh Come All Ye Faithful," which was backed by "Merry Christmas Baby."

Christmas music book in envelope, 1978.
Comes with poster and music sheet.

Christmas music book, 1978.

RCA bonus sticker from the Elvis Sings the Wonderful World of Christmas *album (LSP-4579, 1971).*

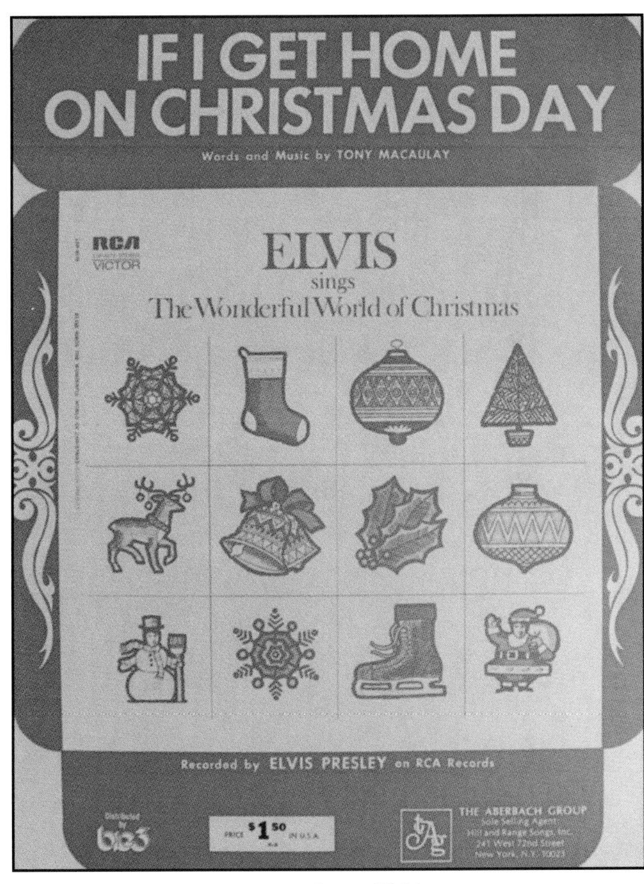

Music sheet, 1971.

Music sheet, 1971.

Music sheet. Part of the Christmas package, 1978.

1965 jukebox record strip of original record.

Special limited edition gold record display
of Elvis's 45rpm single,
"Blue Christmas" / "Santa Claus is Back in Town."

Music sheet, 1980's.

RCA poster used in record stores, 1966.

Brightest Stars of Christmas *album, (RCA DPL1-0086). Made for JC Penney stores, released November 1974. Includes one Elvis song, "Here Comes Santa Claus," side 1, #2.*

Chapter 13
A Star-Studded Christmas

Elvis heard the Charles Brown song "Merry Christmas Baby" for the first time in the early 1950's. Johnny Moore and the Three Blazers recorded it on the Hollywood label in 1947. Elvis liked the song so much that he purchased a copy of the record while in Shreveport, Louisiana, for the Louisiana Hayride. He recorded his own version of the song in May of 1971.

On Christmas Eve 1954, just minutes before his performance at Houston's City Auditorium, singer Johnny Ace shot himself. The circumstances surrounding the bizarre death intrigued Elvis, who did some investigating in an attempt to find out what really happened. It turned out that the singer and some other men had been playing a game of Russian Roulette when the shooting occurred. A short time after his death, Ace's new song, "Pledging My Love," was released on the Duke label. On October 29, 1976, Elvis recorded a version of the same song in honor of Ace.

Every Christmas, Elvis would send Ted Mack a personalized Christmas card. This went on for years, and was the result of Ted Mack's Amateur Hour turning Elvis down as a performer in 1955. Mack said that Elvis was "unfit for public appearance." Elvis was hurt, so he decided that, after he made it big, he would remind Mack every year of what a big mistake he had made in turning him down.

For Christmas 1955, Scotty Moore and his wife Bobbie held a small gathering for their family. After all the gifts had been opened, Scotty sent his sister-in-law, Auzella, and a then 13-year-old Tammy Wynette to deliver gifts to Elvis. The girls were shocked when Elvis himself opened the door of his home located at 1414 Getwell Street. He invited them inside where they shared hot coffee and tea and exchanged gifts. Much later in her life, Wynette recalled how thick and white the carpeting in Elvis's house had been. She also commented on how well Elvis had treated her, making her Christmas very special. He kissed and hugged her several times before she left that day, and she cried all the way back to Scotty's house. Tammy, who became a superstar in her own right, passed away in 1998.

On Christmas Eve 1955, a cold and wet blues songwriter named Otis Blackwell went to the Shalimar Music Company in New York City, where he played seven of his original songs for company executives. The songs were ultimately purchased for $25 each and Otis walked out of the meeting feeling quite proud of himself. He used part of the money to buy himself a pair of galoshes, a big umbrella, and a warm hat.

Shalimar Music Company passed Otis' songs on to Hill & Range Music Company. In July 1956, Hill & Range played a demo version of one of the songs for Elvis, who loved the tune and wanted to record it. He contacted Otis personally and asked if he could have the rights to the song. Although Otis was reluctant, he eventually agreed to the deal. The song was recorded at CBS Studio in New York on January 6, 1957. It took Elvis 50 takes to cut the tune exactly as he wanted it. In the end, Elvis and Otis were listed as partners on the publishing rights. By March of 1992, this recording had gone triple platinum. Otis's song was a little tune called, "Don't Be Cruel."

On December 22, 1956, Elvis made a special appearance at the WDIA Radio Christmas Goodwill Revue benefit held at the Ellis Auditorium in Memphis. Also on the program were B.B. King, Little Junior Parker and Bobby Blue Bland. When Elvis walked out on stage, he greeted all in attendance and wished everyone a very Merry Christmas and a safe and healthy New Year. The young women went crazy and screamed for Elvis. Before Elvis left, program director David James thanked him for his support and appearance. When the benefit was over, Elvis invited the performers and the crew to join him at the Fortune's Jungle Garden, the world's first drive-in restaurant.

When Elvis stopped by Sun Studios to wish owner Sam Phillips a Merry Christmas on December 4, 1956, he was quite amazed to find that an impromptu jam/recording session was taking place with Carl Perkins, Johnny Cash and Jerry Lee Lewis. Elvis was asked to join the session. Phillips quickly took advantage of the situation and recorded the historic session. Known as the "Million Dollar Quartet Session," the event was made into an album of the same title several years later. It includes songs such as "Blueberry Hill," "Islands of Golden Dreams," "I Won't Have to Cross Jordan Alone," "The Old Rugged Cross," and "Down By The Riverside."

Elvis and his backup vocal group, The Jordanaires, visited the Grand Ole Opry on December 21, 1956. Angry at the poor reception he had received at the Opry back in 1954, Elvis was determined to show off his good fortune. As the trip was an impromptu one, Elvis stopped in a Nashville men's store for a new outfit. He purchased a black tuxedo, a white shirt, a bow tie, shoes, and socks. Upon arriving at the Ryman Auditorium, Elvis parked his new white Cadillac at the front door. In attendance at the Opry that night were Faron Young, Johnny Cash, Brenda Lee, and Ray Price, among others. Elvis posed for photos with the performers and offered them his Christmas wishes. He left the Ryman an hour later with renewed confidence, stopping in one of the men's rooms to change his clothes. The newly-purchased tuxedo was thrown into the nearest garbage and Elvis and the Jordanaires returned to Memphis.

Singer Brenda Lee received a wonderful Christmas present on December 21, 1956. Just 13 years old, she was asked to perform at the Grand Ole Opry as part of their Christmas show—and she met the love of her life, Elvis Presley. Both singers were full of compliments for each other, and Brenda was thrilled that a photographer was on hand to document their meeting.

In the 1950's, country singer Miss Bobbie Cryner stated that she and her family were big Elvis fans. She also stated that her family had all of Elvis's albums in their collection. Their favorite was his Christmas album. They had played it every Christmas since 1957.

Sometime in the winter of 1959, entertainer Bob Hope sent members of his staff to Bad Nauheim, Germany, in an attempt to get Elvis to participate in the US Troop Christmas Tour. Elvis politely declined, insisting that he was in the Army to serve and not to sing. When the news of the meeting reached Colonel Parker, he was furious. By that time, everyone knew that all business transactions involving Elvis were to go through him. Elvis was on maneuvers in Grafenwohr and could not be reached, so Parker contacted Hope directly. "Why should Elvis work for the Army for free, when he can get $50,000 for a single night's show?" he demanded. When Hope interrupted to explain that he would indeed pay Elvis to perform, the Colonel was dumbfounded. Not wanting to give the USO troop veteran the advantage, Parker upped Elvis's price to $125,000 and Hope immediately backed off, insisting that he would never pay that much for anyone. Parker was quite pleased with his accomplishment.

At 12:30 p.m. on December 20, 1970, Elvis paid an unscheduled visit to President Richard Nixon. Before arriving at the White House, Elvis went to the Federal Narcotics Bureau and attempted to obtain a narcotics badge. Despite offers of a $5,000 "donation," Elvis's requests were denied by Deputy Director John Finlator. Elvis then approached President Nixon about the matter. Nixon and Elvis immediately took a liking to each other and the President sent a member of his staff to obtain Elvis's narcotics badge. Elvis grabbed Nixon in a bear hug, thanking him repeatedly. At that time he informed the President of his Christmas gift, which was a set of commemorative nickel-plated Colt .45 guns from World War II. Because firearms were not allowed inside the White House, Elvis had been forced to leave the gift outside with the security guard.

In late 1974, Elvis called Karen and Richard Carpenter to tell them that he liked their song, "Merry Christmas Darling," and asked their permission to record the song. The famous duo was thrilled that Elvis liked their song and said they would be honored to have him record it. Unfortunately, Elvis never got around to it because he never recorded another Christmas album.

On Christmas Eve 1975, country singer T.G. Sheppard and his wife Diana visited Elvis at Graceland. Back then, Sheppard was still known by his real name, William Browder, and worked for RCA as a promoter. Browder was not well liked by Elvis's entourage and friends. They thought that Browder came by just to see what he could get because he came over without a gift for Elvis. On this particular night, Elvis decided to take everyone at Graceland for a ride aboard his new airplane, "The Lisa Marie." Elvis asked Browder to bring his wife and come along. Also in attendance was Elvis's jeweler, Lowell Hayes, who had with him a case full of baubles and trinkets. On the plane, Elvis took Lowell into his private bedroom to look over some of the pieces of jewelry. After about an hour, Lowell walked out and told the next person to go in to see Elvis. Elvis then presented that person with his Christmas gift. Elvis was not the type of person to omit anyone present from all the festivities or gift-giving, so in went Browder. He came out with a beautiful ring worth thousands of dollars. Diana, his wife, was also presented with a new ring. Both Browder and his wife thanked Elvis for his generosity and wished him the best, healthiest, and Merriest Christmas of all.

During his December 2-12, 1976, engagement in Las Vegas, Elvis phoned entertainer Wayne Newton. After talking with Newton for over two hours, Elvis invited the singer to attend one of his performances. Although Newton was keenly aware of Elvis's health problems, when Elvis arrived on stage the following evening Newton was shocked by Elvis's appearance and horrified by what he heard. This was not the same man he had grown to love and admire. After the show, Newton went backstage where he looked into his friend's bloodshot eyes and hugged his overweight body. Newton was certain that Elvis's life was slowly slipping away. He quickly offered him his best Christmas wishes and then ran out before Elvis could respond.

Wink Martindale and his wife Sandy visited Elvis right before Christmas in 1976. When the Martindales rose to leave, after several hours of reliving the good ol' days, Elvis begged them to stay a little longer. Years later, both Wink and Sandy recalled that Elvis had been very depressed at the time and seemed desperate to talk to someone from the old days.

In December 1976, Reverend Rex Humbard visited Elvis in his dressing room in Las Vegas. After praying together, Humbard announced that he was going to Jerusalem to prepare Christmas programming. Elvis asked the Reverend to "say a word for me at Calvary."

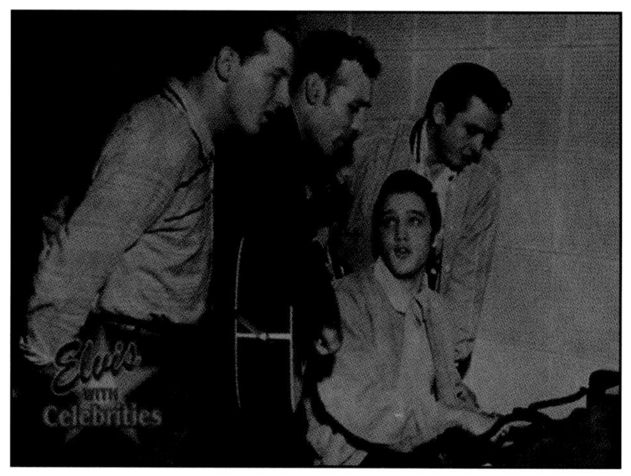

Jerry Lee Lewis, Carl Perkins, Johnny Cash, and Elvis, the "Million Dollar Quartet," December 4, 1957. Card from the Elvis Collection by the River Group, 1992.

Elvis with Brenda Lee, December 20, 1956. Card from the Elvis Collection by the River Group, 1992.

Elvis with Johnny Cash, December 20, 1956. Card from the Elvis Collection by the River Group, 1992.

Christmas ornament, 1990's.

Elvis and the Colonel meet with Tennessee Governor Frank Clements at the Grand Ole Opry in Nashville, Tennessee, on December 20, 1956.

Elvis with legend Hank Snow at the Grand Ole Opry, December 20, 1956.

Elvis with country singer Faron Young, Grand Ole Opry, December 20, 1956.

At the Grand Ole Opry on December 20, 1956. Elvis is second from left. At far left is John Denny. Second from right is Ray Price.

Ferlin Huskey, Elvis, Faron Young, Hawkshaw Hawkins, and John Denny, backstage at the Grand Ole Opry, December 20, 1956.

Elvis with the Wilburn Brothers, Teddy and Doyle. Grand Ole Opry, December 20, 1956.

Christmas ornament, 1990's.

Elvis with entertainers Sergio Mendez and Paul Anka at Caesar's Palace in Las Vegas, December 1972.

Special album released by Avon Products in 1985 (DPLI-0716).
Features Elvis's "Silver Bells."

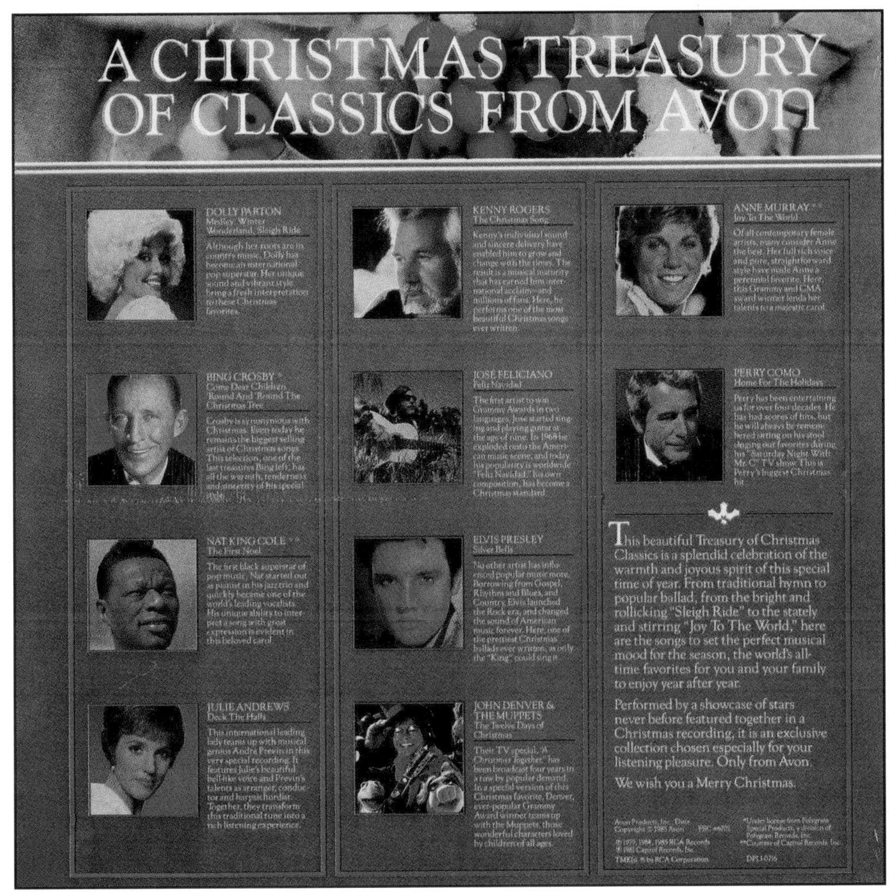

Back cover of the special Avon Christmas album released in 1985
featuring Elvis's "Silver Bells."

RCA Las Vegas postcard, early 1970's.

Chapter 14
Christmas in Vegas

The Colonel dressed as Santa Claus on April 1, 1975. With Elvis's chow dog Getlow in tow, Parker surprised Elvis on stage during one of his concerts. To the delight of the audience, the band played "Jingle Bells" as Parker and the dog pranced around the stage. The Colonel received a standing ovation for his April Fool's Day practical joke as he walked off the stage Ho-Ho-Ho-ing!

An opening night package was handed out to 2,000 special guests at Elvis's concert on December 2, 1975, at the Hilton. Inside the envelope, which sported Christmas drawings in the upper left hand corner, each guest found the new Elvis menu, a pocket calendar, a photo postcard, a drawing, a scarf, a mini photo album, and a Christmas postcard featuring Elvis with Santa Claus. For the duration of Elvis's engagement, which ran until December 15th, the fans were able to purchase similar special souvenir packages adorned with the words "Special Souvenir Package" at a cost of $3.

The late Andy Kern, an Elvis memorabilia collector, once stated that his most prized possession was an unopened copy of *Elvis' Christmas Album* (LOC-1035). In 1975, the record was worth $1,000. Kern met Elvis backstage at the Hilton hotel that year and asked his idol to sign the precious album. Elvis was more than happy to accommodate Kern and he immediately tore open the record, tossing the poly-wrap into a nearby trash can. Kern was aghast but said nothing to Elvis, who had just mutilated his collector's item! In the end, the album became worth even more because of Elvis's signature.

When Elvis was forced to cancel several shows at the Hilton Hotel in Las Vegas in August of 1975, the concerts were rescheduled for December. Although the months of November and December were typically the slowest time of the year for the hotel and casino, Elvis's appearances were sold out. Happy with the business, Henri Lewin approached Colonel Parker and asked if it were possible to continue the run through the new year. Parker explained that Elvis would not spend the holiday away from Graceland and that he already had a show scheduled for December 31 at the Pontiac Silverdome. Lewin's offer was rejected.

On December 5, 1976, Elvis took a fall in his hotel room, spraining his ankle. He did not cancel any of his shows, however, choosing instead to perform while sitting on a stool. He was trying to do all his crazy moves from a sitting position and some of them looked rather funny. At the end of each show the audience gave Elvis a standing ovation in appreciation of his doing the shows in spite of his injury.

Fan club Christmas greeting card.

Fan photo greeting card.

RCA bonus postcard from the LP Elvis Sings the Wonderful World of Christmas. *(1971)*

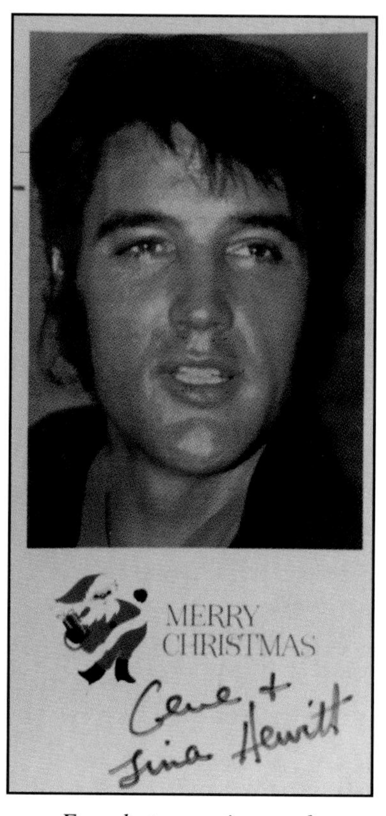

Fan photo greeting card.

Fan photo greeting card.

Fan club Christmas greeting card.

Fan club Christmas greeting card.

1971 Las Vegas postcard from RCA.

Elvis receives a New Musical Express award from his British fan club, Las Vegas, December 1973.

Ad for Elvis's opening night show on December 2, 1975, called the "Pre-Holiday Jubilee." The ad ran in Vegas Visitor *and* Now *magazines.*

Elvis shows the audience at the Las Vegas Hilton the toy Santa a fan gave to him, December 1974.

Banner that hung on the walls of the Las Vegas Hilton Hotel to promote Elvis's Christmas engagement in 1975.

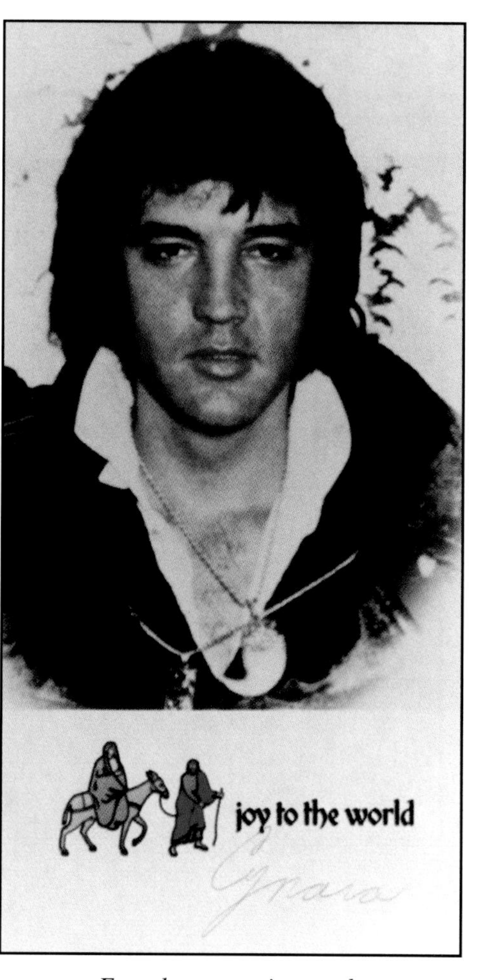

Fan photo greeting card.

During Elvis's April 1, 1975, show in Las Vegas, the Colonel donned a Santa suit and walked on stage to play an April Fool's gag on Elvis.

Christmas engagement at the Las Vegas Hilton Hotel, December 13, 1975.

Las Vegas placemat. Came in red and green with a metallic background.

December 13, 1975, Las Vegas Hilton.

During Elvis's Las Vegas Hilton Hotel Christmas engagement, December 15, 1975.

Elvis hugs a giant Snoopy stuffed animal on stage on December 15, 1975, at the Las Vegas Hilton.

December 15, 1975, Las Vegas Hilton.

December 15, 1975, Las Vegas Hilton.

December 1975 issue of Vegas Visitor *magazine, promoting Elvis's Christmas engagement.*

Very rare holiday souvenir package from Las Vegas Hilton Hotel, December 2-15, 1975. Contains mini poster, mini tour book, Christmas postcard, Christmas pocket calendar, fold-out poster, tour photo, wall menu, souvenir menu, and 1975 Hilton postcard.

Las Vegas Hilton in-house magazine, promoting Elvis's December 5-12, 1975, appearances. (December 1975)

Las Vegas poster promoting Elvis's Pre-Holiday concerts, which hung in the Hitlon Hotel during November and December, 1975.

December 15, 1975, Las Vegas Hilton.

December 11, 1976, midnight show at the Vegas Hilton.

December 12, 1976, Las Vegas Hilton.

December 12, 1976, Vegas Hilton.

December 12, 1976, Vegas Hilton.

December 13, 1976, midnight show at the Hilton.

December 13, 1976,Vegas show.

December 14, 1976, Vegas Hilton.

December 14, 1976, Vegas Hilton.

RCA postcard from Las Vegas, 1974.

Elvis Santa Christmas greeting card, Great Britain.
Illustration by Leon Garcia.

Chapter 15
A Very Funny Christmas

Elvis always bought fireworks to celebrate the Christmas holidays. On December 26, 1960, Elvis found a leftover roman candle, which he lit and shot at his Uncle Earl. The flaming ball hit Uncle Earl's jacket and set it on fire. Elvis was in hysterics as he watched his uncle run around in circles trying to pull the jacket off.

One Christmas, Elvis accidentally shot a rocket through the window of the den at Graceland. Several guests had gathered in the room and as the rocket shattered the window they screamed and ducked for cover. The rocket zipped all around the room and at the end of its course, landed in the Christmas cake, splattering the sweet confection in all directions. Out on the lawn, Elvis was in hysterics. He fell to the ground and laughed so hard that he split his pants wide open!

One Christmas in the mid-1960's, Elvis decided to go out on his own to get the Christmas tree for Graceland. He took his new Rolls Royce as he toured Memphis, searching for the perfect tree. He spotted one he liked, and as he was pulling over to the side of the road, his car slipped on the ice and plowed into a snow bank. As there was nothing he could do about the car, Elvis hiked back to Graceland, dragging the tree behind him. When he arrived home he tripped on some boxes in the foyer and went sprawling head first with the tree landing on top of him. Finally, he had the tree positioned exactly as he wanted it and he began to decorate it. The tree was so tall that Elvis had to use a step ladder to place decorations on the top branches. When he was on the ladder, his collie, Sheba, knocked him down. To make matters worse, when Elvis finally finished decorating the tree and plugged in the lights, a fuse blew! A frustrated Elvis retreated to his room and did not come back downstairs until his men had fixed the tree, restored the power, and retrieved his stranded car.

Elvis owned a pet chimpanzee called Scatter who loved both women and booze. During one of Elvis's Christmas parties in the early 1960's, he decided that Scatter should attend. Dee Stanley, Vernon's second wife, had been given the task of dressing the chimp for the occasion. As Dee proceeded to put a dressy sports jacket on Scatter, he bit down on her finger and would not let go. Startled by the pain, Dee was unable to speak, and many of the guests in attendance thought that she was laughing at the chimp's antics. Elvis was the first to realize that the woman was crying, and he promptly punched Scatter and sent him reeling. Elvis then took Dee to the hospital where she was given a rabies shot. After that incident Scatter was kept locked up any time Elvis had a party.

During one of Elvis's Christmas parties in the mid-1960's, the man whom Elvis designated as the punch-maker decided to spice up the punch with not one (as he was instructed) but four bottles of vodka. He also threw in a bottle of wine to give the drink some color. Elvis noticed his guests' strange reaction to the punch and soon realized what had happened. He became hysterical as he watched their pained expressions after downing the toxic mixture. Elvis congratulated the punch-maker, thanking him for starting the party off right.

In 1965, Elvis decided to dress up as Santa Claus and go to the Whitehaven Shopping Center to spread some holiday cheer. He found a chair, sat in the middle of the center, and soon had children sitting on his lap and telling him what they most wanted for Christmas. When some heavier children approached, Elvis heard his men begin to laugh. Elvis tried hard to control his own laughter, as he did not want to hurt the children's feelings. Soon, Elvis couldn't take it anymore. He quickly excused himself and ran from the shopping center before anyone could see him laughing. On the way back to Graceland, Elvis and his bodyguards had a good laugh over Elvis's attempt to portray Santa Claus.

On Christmas Day in 1967, Elvis and Priscilla were the recipients of gag gifts from their friends. Elvis received an old, worn out suitcase and Priscilla got a pair of underwear large enough for a 250-pound woman. Elvis joked that if the pregnant Priscilla didn't watch out, she'd soon fit into her new underwear. Priscilla told her husband that if he didn't watch it, he would be making good use of that tattered suitcase. Everyone present applauded the Presleys for their quick wit.

One Christmas in the 1970's, Elvis decided to play a joke on his family and friends. He went to the local McDonald's and purchased dozens of their 50-cent gift certificates. When the time came to exchange gifts at Graceland, Elvis passed out the envelopes one by one. He made sure that each person understood that this was to be their only gift, while informing them that money had been a little tight that year. He delighted in their confused expressions as they opened the envelopes and saw the fast food gift certificates inside. Everyone knew that Elvis had made close to $4 million that year, and could not understand what was going on. When Elvis decided they had had enough, he let them in on the joke and gave them their real presents — envelopes filled with money!

In the middle to late 1970's, Elvis was known to frequent a popular ski resort directly before or just after Christmas Day. The funny thing about the trips, which included any and all friends who wanted to come along, was that Elvis did not know how to ski, nor did he wish to learn. He went solely for the snowmobiling and snowball fights. While at the resort Elvis always wore a ski mask which covered his entire face and prevented him from being recognized. His men made fun of the mask, calling Elvis "the snow creature" and pelting him with snowballs. Elvis enjoyed these "fights" and participated in them wholeheartedly.

Elvis puts a Santa hat on Charlie Hodge while on stage at the Las Vegas Hilton Hotel during Christmas 1974.

Elvis laughs at a joke while holding the Santa hat that only moments before was on Charlie Hodge's head. Vegas Hilton, December 1974.

Amusing pinback button featuring Santa and Elvis dwarves (1990's).

A funny Elvis puts on all of the Christmas gifts he received from fans, December 13, 1975 (Las Vegas Hilton).

A comical-looking Elvis makes everyone laugh at the Las Vegas Hilton on December 13, 1975.

THIS PAGE
IS
DEDICATED
TO
ELVIS

WITH OUR LOVE
AND
MEMORIES
FOREVER.

THE
ELVIS
FANS
FROM
HOOSIERLAND
FAN
CLUB.

ELVIS FOREVER

(2)

Peanuts comic strip regarding Christmas and Elvis, 1980's.

Amusing Elvis T-shirt, 1990's.

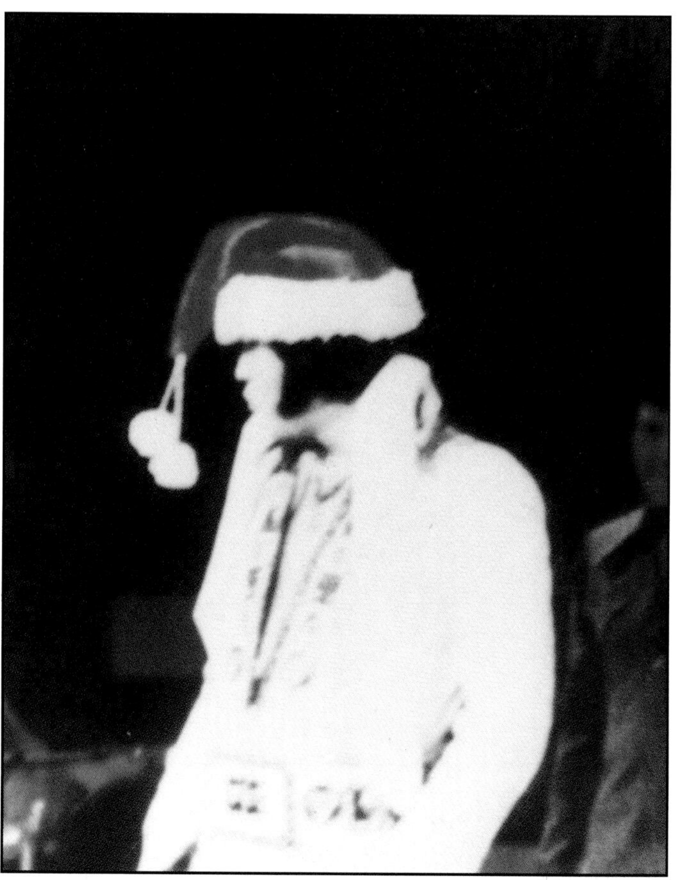

December 14, 1976. Elvis wears one of the Santa hats given to him by a fan.

Fan photo greeting card.

Elvis receives yet another Santa hat from a fan. December 11, 1976, Las Vegas Hilton.

Elvis and Charlie Hodge share a public display of hysteria as Charlie holds the microphone for Elvis. Elvis had sprained his ankle and was forced to do the entire show sitting on a stool. December 11, 1976, Las Vegas Hilton.

'Twas the night before Christmas
and all through the shack,
I could hear the distinct sounds
of my Grandpappy's hack.

We had just hung our stockings
in a jubilant mood,
in hopes that St. Elvis
would bring us some food.

Daddy was nestled
all snug in his bed,
coal dust covering
his pillow and head.

No wood in the stove,
the cold numbed my feet,
to add insult to injury,
Ol' Red was in heat.

When out on the lawn
I heard the grinding of gears,
I sprang from my bed
almost frightened to tears.

When what to my wondering
eyes should appear,
but a miniature sleigh
pulled by a dark green John Deere.

With a little ol' driver
shaking his pelvis,
I instantly knew that
it must be St. Elvis.

Funny Christmas greeting card (front).

He was dressed all in sequins
from his head to his toes,
and the top of his lip
curled up to his nose.

His hips how they twitched,
his gut was titanic,
when he leaned on the porch rail,
I went into a panic.

Huffing and puffing,
his face turning red,
soon gave me to know,
he'd come back from the dead.

He sang not a note,
but went straight to his work,
filled all the stockings
and turned with a jerk.

Then hitching his pants,
lumbered back to the sleigh,
fired up the tractor,
and was soon on his way.

Then he bid us adieu
with his personal touch...

"Merry Christmas to all
and Thanks Veramuch!"

Funny Christmas greeting card (inside).

December 30, 1976, Omni Arena, Atlanta, Georgia.

Funny Christmas greeting postcard by Alfred Gescheidt.

RCA Christmas postcard, 1971/1972.

Chapter 16
A Christmas Tour

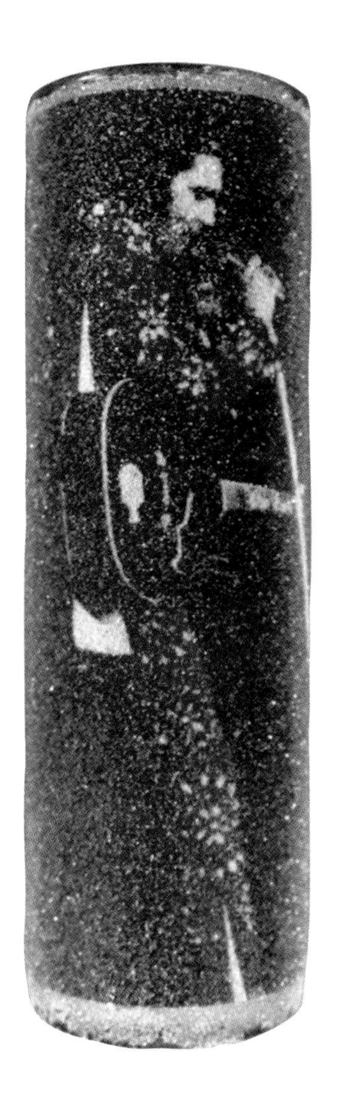
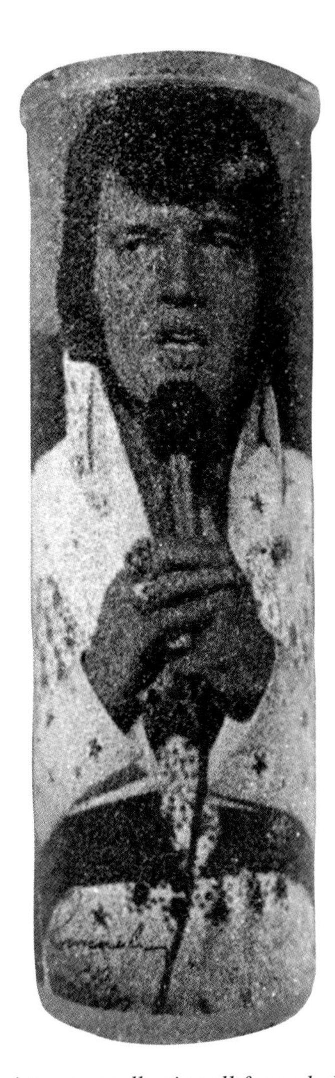

Christmas candles in tall frosted glasses.

Fan photo greeting card.

Fan photo greeting card.

Fan photo greeting card.

Fan photo greeting card.

Fan photo greeting card.

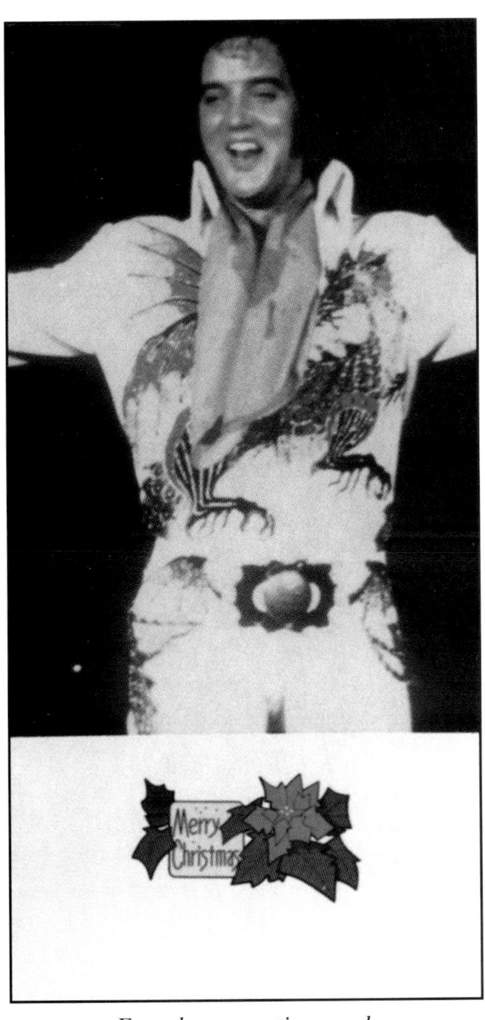

Fan photo greeting card.

Fan photo greeting card.

Fan club Christmas greeting card.

At the Henry Levitt Arena in Wichita, Kansas, December 27, 1976.

Fan club Christmas greeting card.

Advertisement from fan club brochure.

Fan photo greeting card.

Christmas candles in tall frosted glasses.

Fan photo greeting card.

Fan photo greeting card.

Fan photo greeting card.

Fan photo greeting card.

Omni Arena, Atlanta, Georgia, December 30, 1976.

Fan club Christmas greeting card.

Omni Arena, Atlanta, Georgia, December 30, 1976.

Omni Arena, Atlanta, Georgia, December 30, 1976.

Fan club Christmas greeting card.

Fan photo greeting card.

RCA Christmas postcard from 1975.

RCA Christmas postcard, 1961.

Chapter 17
Memories of Christmas

Around Christmastime in 1955, Steve Sholes, the RCA executive who was responsible for signing Elvis with RCA, called guitarist Chet Atkins. Atkins was an RCA session guitarist at that time and he and Sholes discussed the possibility of getting a band together within a week's time. Atkins wanted to know why a band was needed and when Sholes told him about Elvis, Atkins told him that he would need a week. Atkins hand-picked each musician. On piano was Floyd Cramer. Murray "Buddy" Harmen was on drums, and the Jordanaires were the vocal backup. Since Elvis already had Scotty Moore on guitar and Bill Black on bass, Atkins did not need to find replacements for them.

Scotty Moore and Bill Black had their worst Christmas ever in 1956. They were flat broke and could barely support their families. They could not buy gifts because of the lack of money. They prayed long and hard that Christmas for more money and more work.

When Elvis was contracted to do *GI Blues*, the original working title was *Christmas in Berlin*. The original script was different from the one Elvis used. This script was about a soldier named Memphis who was stationed in West Berlin, Germany. Memphis had a dream about opening his own nightclub in Brooklyn, New York. By the time Elvis started filming the movie, the script had been rewritten and the movie re-titled. Elvis played Tulsa McLean, a soldier stationed in Frankfurt, Germany. Tulsa had dreams of transforming a chili parlor in Oklahoma into a hot-spot nightclub. Elvis was more interested in the original script and asked Paramount Studios if they could do the film with it. Wallis said no because he felt the new script was better suited to Elvis.

Holiday movie ad for G.I. Blues.
From Motion Picture Exhibitor *magazine, November 16, 1960.*

Fan club Christmas greeting card.

Holiday movie ad for Flaming Star.
From Motion Picture Exhibitor *magazine, 1960.*

Fan photo greeting card.

Newpaper ad promoting a Christmas holiday movie theatre schedule.

Fan club mini greeting card.

Fan club greeting card.

Fan club Christmas card.

Fan club greeting card, 1962.

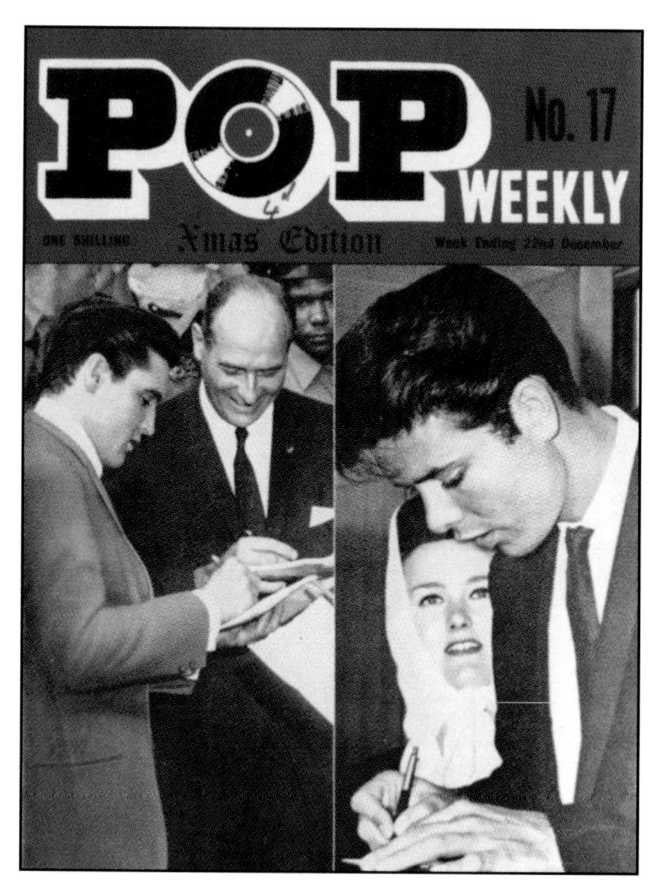

Special Christmas edition of England's Pop *magazine. #17, December 22, 1962.*

Hallmark greeting card. Photo inserted by fan club.

Fan club greeting card.

Fan photo greeting card.

Fan club greeting card.

Newspaper ad for the running of Elvis's Clambake *at the Rialto Theater, Christmas 1967.*

Fan club Christmas greeting card, Great Britain.

Fan photo greeting card.

RCA special bonus postcard from the
Memories of Christmas *album, 1982-1983.*

1966 RCA postcard was a special giveaway from record stores that sold Elvis's RCA Christmas records. 5 1/2" x 8 1/2" in size.

Fan club Christmas postcard, "Elvis Presley Underground," mid-1960's.

Chapter 18
A Fan Club Christmas

In 1957, Elvis sent his Christmas wishes to his fans in the United Kingdom via a cable telegram. The telegram read: "My sincere best wishes to all of the members of my fan club for a Merry Christmas and a Happy New Year, and I hope that in the coming year, you will be blessed as I have. Colonel Parker and Tom Diskin send you all their sincere best wishes also." It was signed "Elvis."

Depressed about the loss of his mother and about his father dating another woman, Elvis was not in a happy mood on Christmas Day, 1960 although he was happy that he was out of the Army and that his house looked great with all the Christmas lights. He invited several of the fans waiting at the gates up to the house. He was nearly trampled when they ran inside pushing past him, not wanting to chance a change of mind. Elvis, not expecting this response, could do nothing else but welcome them. He held a little party and offered everyone food and drinks and even gave the group a tour of his home. Everyone was on their best behavior and, when the evening ended, they all wished him a great Christmas!

When Elvis found out that one of his United Kingdom fan club members, a thirteen-year-old girl, was ill with polio, he sent her a special Christmas message. His telegram read:

"For your little honorary member: a very Merry Christmas and a Happy New Year. I hope and pray that you will make a speedy recovery and I am very proud to have you for a fan and a friend. Your pal, Elvis."

The young girl cried as the fan club president read the cable from Elvis.

Elvis bought 36 transistor radios to give to his friends and relatives for Christmas in 1960. As he was wrapping the gifts, he glanced at the closed circuit TV and noticed one of his fan club presidents at the gates. He went down to meet her, and ended up presenting her with one of the radios. As the two were chatting, another girl approached and boldly asked, "Please, Elvis, may I have one too?" Pretty soon, Elvis had given away ten of the radios! The following day, Elvis received a letter which read: "I don't want to be nosy, but I understand you are giving away transistor radios for Christmas. Did you inadvertently forget my daughter?" Elvis was furious. He could not believe that this woman was attempting to force him to give someone a Christmas gift. He never responded to her letter and gave his men instructions to keep her away from his property.

Gary Pepper and his Tankers Fan Club bought Elvis a very special Christmas gift in 1961: a gas-powered go-cart. When Gary and his father delivered the present, Elvis immediately took it for a spin around the driveway. It turned out to be one of Elvis's favorite Christmas gifts.

During the Christmas holidays in 1961, Elvis meets with Albert Hand, publisher of The Elvis Monthly, *on the set of* Kid Galahad.

1965 fan club publication, "Golden Platters Fan Club."

1960's fan club Christmas postcard, "The King Creole Elvis Prelsey Fan Club," South Africa.

Elvis Presley Golden Platters fan club publication.

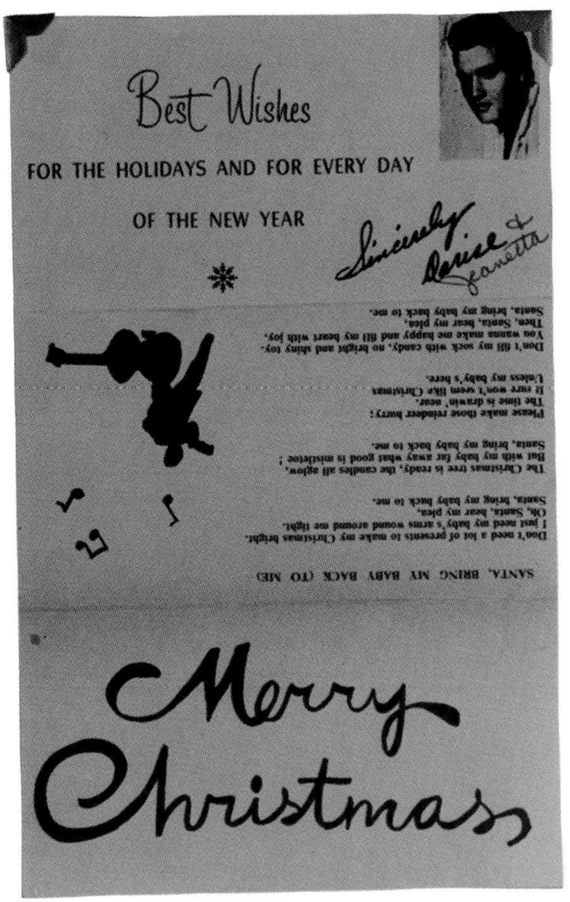

Folded fan club Christmas note bearing the lyrics to Elvis's "Santa Bring My Baby Back to Me."

1961 Christmas postcard from The Loyal's Presley fan club of Hawaii.

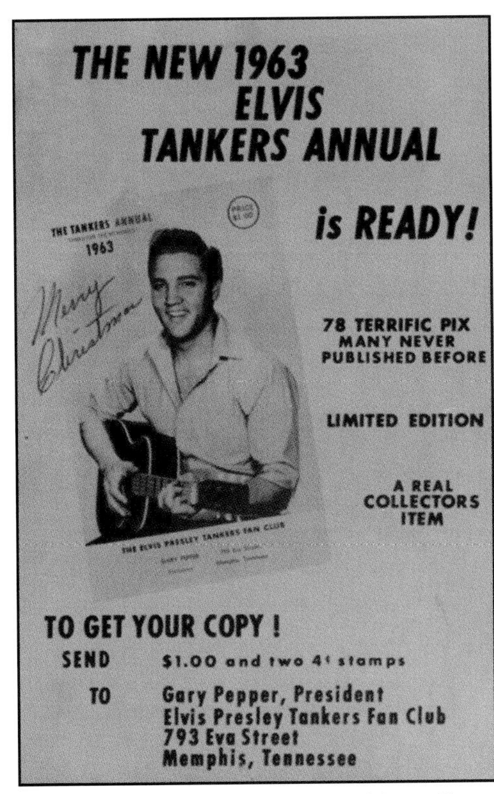

Flyer promoting the new annual from Gary Pepper's Tankers fan club, Christmas 1963.

1964 fan club Christmas postcard, "Our King Fan Club."

Christmas card from the Netherlands, mid-1960's.

Inside the Christmas card from the Netherlands.

Het Bestuur van de
Nederlandse
Elvis Presley Fanclub
wenst u
Prettige Kerstdagen
en een
in alle opzichten zeer
Voorspoedig Nieuwjaar

Dec. 1968 / Jan. 1969 fan club publication from New Zealand, "The Official Kiwi Elvis Presley Fan Club."

Late 1960's fan club Christmas postcard, "Hound Dogs Elvis Fan Club."

Early 1970's fan club Christmas postcard,
"Official Independent Association Elvis Presley Fan Club."

1991 fan club publication from Greece,
"Elvis Forever Fan Club,"

1984 fan club publication,
"The Wonder of You Elvis Presley Fan Club."

Fan club photo.

Nov./Dec. 1973 fan club publication, "The Elvis Generation."

December 1971 fan club publication from England, "Elvis Monthly."

Fan club booklet from "The Strictly Elvis Generation," dated Nov./Dec. 1977.

Dec. 1978 / Jan. 1979 fan club publication,
"Taking Care of Elvis."

Dec. 1979 / Jan. 1980 fan club publication,
"Taking Care of Elvis."

1979 fan club publication from Norway,
"Flaming Star."

1979 fan club publication from Norway.

1980 fan club publication magazine from Norway, "A Legendary Performer."

Dec. 1979 / Jan. 1980 fan club publication/magazine, "Elvis the Record."

Oct./Nov./Dec. 1988 fan club publication from China, "International Elvis Presley Fan Club."

Elvis 10 YEARS AFTER

THE NATIONAL ELVIS PRESLEY FAN CLUB MAGAZINE

January 1988

January 1988 fan club publication, "The National Elvis Presley Fan Club," from The Official Elvis Presley Fan Club of Great Britain.

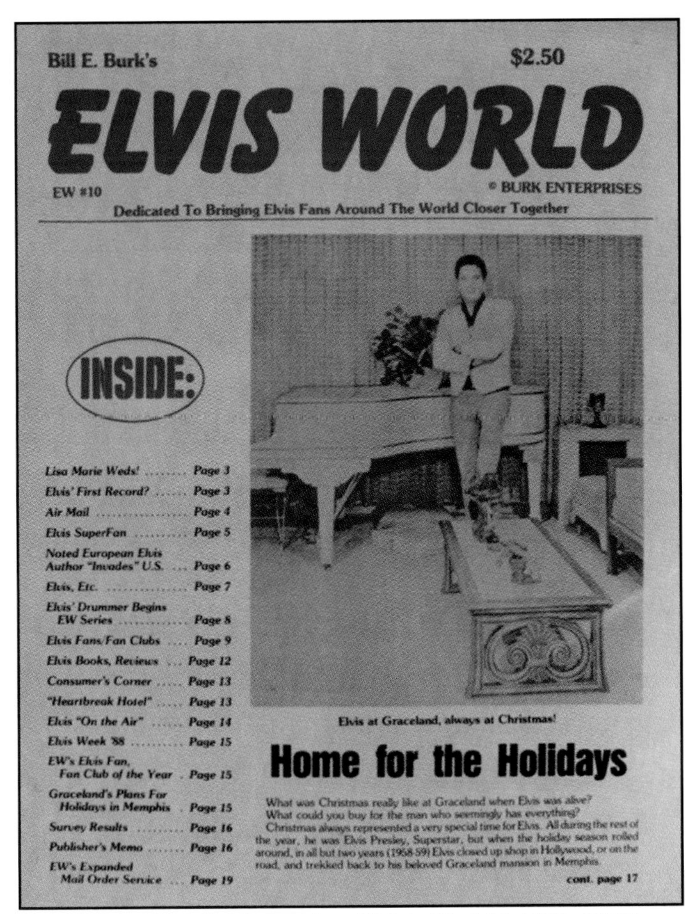

Bill E. Burk's $2.50

ELVIS WORLD

EW #10 © BURK ENTERPRISES

Dedicated To Bringing Elvis Fans Around The World Closer Together

INSIDE:

Elvis at Graceland, always at Christmas!

Home for the Holidays

What was Christmas really like at Graceland when Elvis was alive? What could you buy for the man who seemingly has everything?

Christmas always represented a very special time for Elvis. All during the rest of the year, he was Elvis Presley, Superstar, but when the holiday season rolled around, in all but two years (1958-59) Elvis closed up shop in Hollywood, or on the road, and trekked back to his beloved Graceland mansion in Memphis.

cont. page 17

Fan club publication/magazine, "Elvis World." (#10, 1988)

ELVIS

THAT'S THE WAY IT IS

ISSUE-17 NOV.-DEC '88

Happy Holidays

FAN CLUB OF CHICAGO, ILLINOIS

Nov./Dec. 1988 fan club publication, "Elvis—That's the Way It Is."

Elvis

ELVIS MAIL HOLIDAY EXTRA

1991 fan club publication from The Official Elvis Presley Fan Club of Great Britain.

1991 fan club publication, "Elvis International Forum."

Dec. 1992 / Jan. 1993 fan club publication, "The Official Elvis Presley Organisation in Great Britain."

December 1996 fan club publication, "The Official Elvis Presley Fan Club of Sweden."

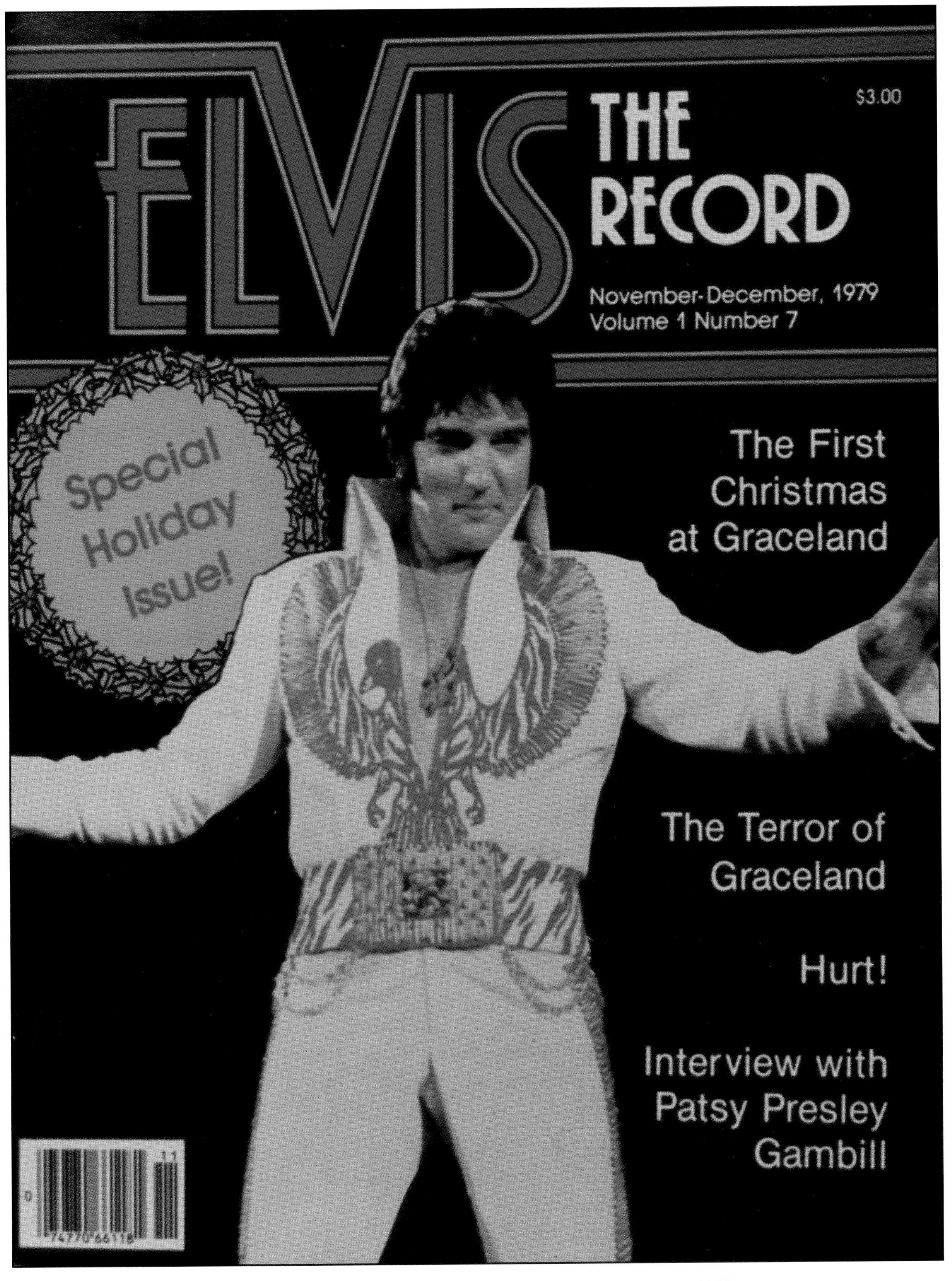

Fan club publication/magazine Elvis The Record, *Nov/Dec 1979.*

Fan photo greeting card.

Chapter 19
A Blue Christmas Without Elvis

When Elvis died, he was buried in the outfit that Vernon had given him for Christmas in 1976. It was a white suit with a blue shirt and a silver tie. Since it was his last Christmas gift to his son, Vernon thought that dressing Elvis in it was appropriate, although it saddened him to dress his son in what was meant to be a happy and joyous gift for Christmas.

WABC radio in New York aired a special four-hour program called "Elvis-A World of Music and Friends" in the fall of 1977. On the program, Priscilla recalled her past Christmases at Graceland. She said that she and Elvis had a lot of fun decorating the tree in the dining room. This special was aired again in 1985.

On December 19, 1977, Memphis held its annual Christmas Liberty Bowl football game. During half-time, the Memphis Symphony Orchestra performed several Elvis songs for the audience. There was a fireworks display during which all 50,000 in attendance waved their US flags as Elvis's "American Trilogy" was played throughout the stadium.

During Christmas in 1977, Donald Lancaster Photography in Memphis sold special Christmas cards of a photo which depicted Graceland with all its Christmas lights and decorations. The box, containing twenty cards and envelopes, sold for $8.00.

The Colonel stated that the sales of the "Always Elvis," "Portrait of Elvis," and "The Golden Years of Elvis" wines dropped considerably during the Christmas holidays in 1979. He was quoted as saying, "Christmas interfered a bit!" After the holidays, sales were back to normal.

In 1988, artist Ralph Wolfe Cowen created a painting entitled "Praying Elvis." The portrait depicted Elvis in profile, dressed in a white suit with his hands folded in prayer. Against a background of puffy clouds, a halo can be seen around Elvis's head. The Graceland estate used the painting on Christmas cards which were sold at their souvenir shops. The interior of the card read: "A gentle prayer for Christmas / A gentle prayer of love / All my fondest wishes / Coming from above."

Bumper sticker.

First day issue of the 20th anniversary Elvis' Christmas Album *Gold Record, November 1957. Postmarked December 25, 1977.*

Satin Christmas ball, Factors, Inc., 1977.

Cardboard store display for the Elvis satin Christmas ball, 1977.

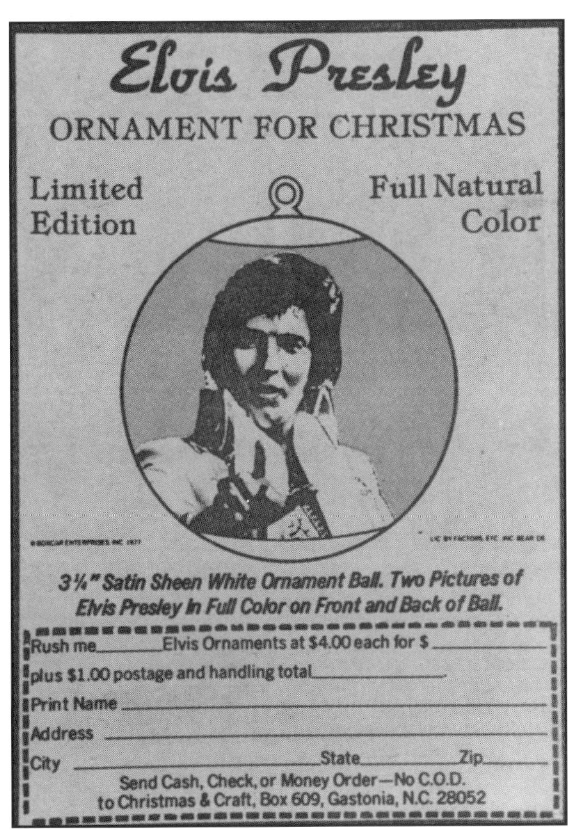

Newspaper ad and mail-in coupon for the Elvis white satin Christmas ball.

Elvis Christmas tree topper.

Christmas stocking by Topperscot.

Christmas greeting card which shows the famous bronze statue of Elvis located on Beale Street in Memphis.

Ticket stub from the "Christmas with Elvis '79 Convention," in Baltimore, Maryland, on December 12, 1979.

Ceramic Christmas ball made for the Elvis Presley Memorial Dinner, 1980's.

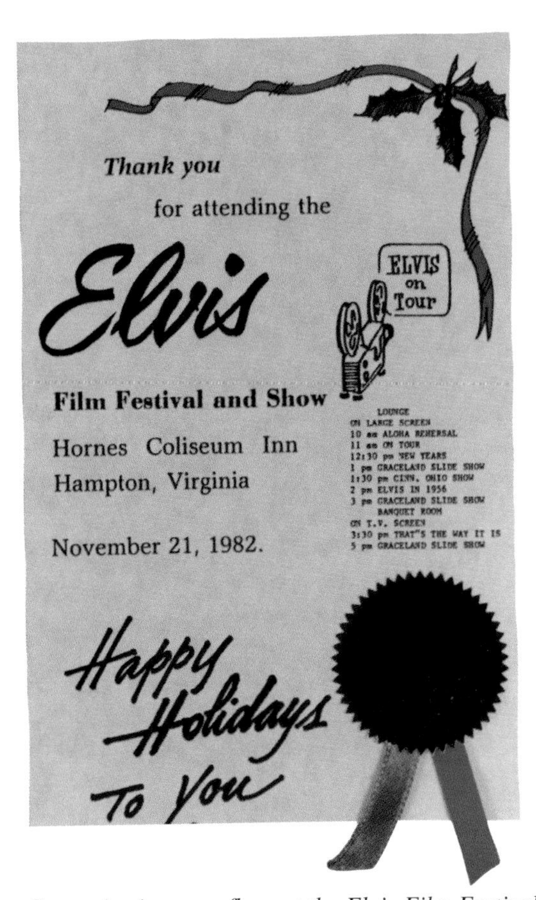

Souvenir giveaway flyer at the Elvis Film Festival & Show in Hampton, Virginia, November 21, 1982.

Hallmark keepsake Christmas ornament. A Gold Crown exclusive, brass plated and dated 1992.

Hallmark keepsake ornament, 1992.

"The Official Elvis Presley 1992 Ornament Collection." Beautiful brass ornaments in a white box, by Elvis Presley Enterprises.

Special Christmas issue of Song Hits Magazine, *"Elvis Special Collectors Series," Winter 1987, by Jim Curtin.*

Beautiful brass ornaments from the "Official Elvis Presley 1992 Christmas Ornament Collection."

Certificate of Authenticity

This is to certify that

"Heartbreak Hotel" and "Jailhouse Rock"

are the first set in the *Solid Gold Elvis Heirloom Porcelain* Ornament Collection.

Each fine collectible is strictly limited to 95 firing days and is crafted to meet or exceed the strictest quality standards of The Bradford Editions.

J. Marie Korth
Director

Number

The Bradford Editions

1999 set of Solid Gold Elvis Heirloom Porcelain Ornaments by the Bradford Exchange. "Heartbreak Hotel" and "Jailhouse Rock."

Hanging Christmas ornament by Presents, 1991.

Carlton Cards musical Christmas ornament #1.
Plays the song, "Blue Christmas."

Carlton Cards ornament #1.

Carlton Cards musical Christmas ornament #2, 1996.
Plays the song, "Santa Bring My Baby Back (To Me)."

Carlton Cards ornament #2.

Carlton Cards musical Christmas ornament #3, 1997. Plays the songs, "Here Comes Santa Claus" and "Winter Wonderland."

Carlton Cards ornament #3.

Elvis guitar Christmas ornament by American Greetings, late 1990's.

Christmas ornament commemorating the 20th anniversary of Elvis's death, 1997. By Topperscot, Inc.

1992 Graceland Christmas greeting card sent to family, friends, and fans. Includes an invitation to the unveiling of the Elvis stamp at Graceland.

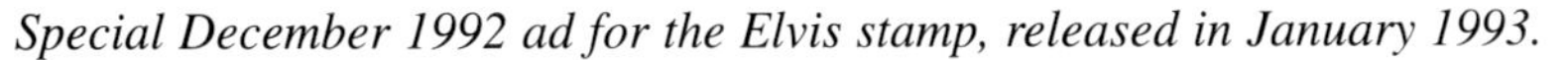

Special December 1992 ad for the Elvis stamp, released in January 1993.

Special Elvis stamp Christmas ornament.

*Special collector's plate of Graceland at Christmastime.
Made in Japan.*

Chapter 20
Christmas at Graceland

Graceland Christmas ornament.

Christmas postcard of Graceland, 1987.

The Graceland gates at Christmastime.

Christmas candle in tall frosted glass.

Christmas pinback button with ribbons, 1982.

Christmas postcard of Graceland, 1987.

Christmas postcard, 1992.

Graceland Christmas ball ornament, 1990's.

Christmas 1982.

The Nativity set.

Christmas at Graceland.

Christmas 1983.

Graceland at night, Christmas 1982.

At night, Christmas 1982.

The nativity set at Graceland.

Christmas 1982.

Graceland during Christmas, 1983.

Christmas 1982.

The lobby of Elvis's raquetball court, Christmas 1983.

Dining room at Graceland, Christmas 1983.

Dining room at Graceland, Christmas 1983.

Dining room at Graceland, Christmas 1983. The Christmas tree is still located in the same spot as when Elvis was alive.

The stairs at Graceland lined with white poinsettias, Christmas 1985.

The living room at Graceland, Christmas 1985.

Dining room at Graceland, Christmas 1985.

Christmas 1988.

Living room at Graceland, Christmas 1988.

Christmas 1988. Full-size Christmas tree in the lobby of Elvis's racquetball court.

GRACELAND NEWS

"CHRISTMAS AT GRACELAND"

PLANS FOR GRACELAND 1983

Graceland newspaper, Winter 1982.

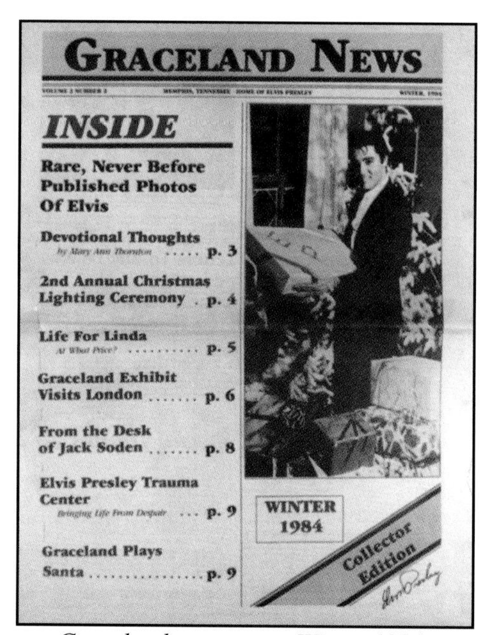
GRACELAND NEWS

INSIDE

Rare, Never Before Published Photos Of Elvis

Devotional Thoughts ..... p. 3

2nd Annual Christmas Lighting Ceremony . p. 4

Life For Linda .... p. 5

Graceland Exhibit Visits London .... p. 6

From the Desk of Jack Soden .... p. 8

Elvis Presley Trauma Center ... p. 9

Graceland Plays Santa .... p. 9

WINTER 1984

Collector Edition

Graceland newspaper, Winter 1984.

Christmas ornament from Graceland, 1990's.

Christmas 1988.

Graceland Gift Catalog, Fall 1990.

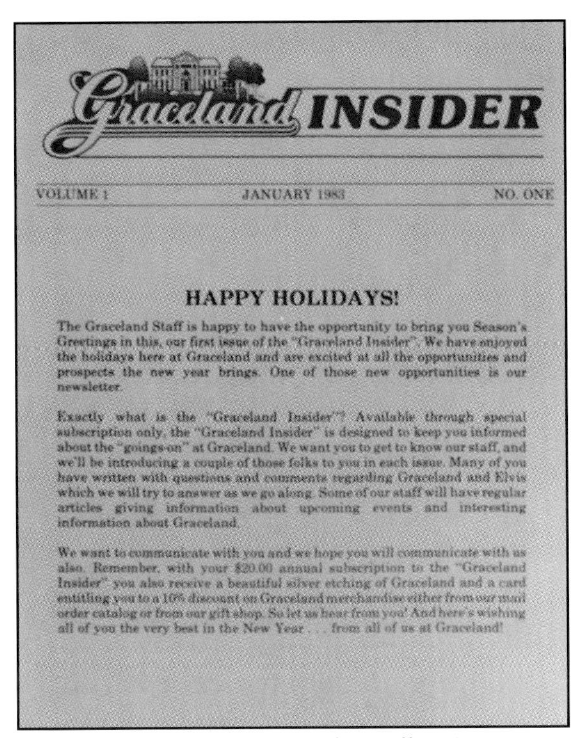

Graceland INSIDER

VOLUME 1 JANUARY 1983 NO. ONE

HAPPY HOLIDAYS!

The Graceland Staff is happy to have the opportunity to bring you Season's Greetings in this, our first issue of the "Graceland Insider". We have enjoyed the holidays here at Graceland and are excited at all the opportunities and prospects the new year brings. One of those new opportunities is our newsletter.

Exactly what is the "Graceland Insider"? Available through special subscription only, the "Graceland Insider" is designed to keep you informed about the "goings-on" at Graceland. We want you to get to know our staff, and we'll be introducing a couple of those folks to you in each issue. Many of you have written with questions and comments regarding Graceland and Elvis which we will try to answer as we go along. Some of our staff will have regular articles giving information about upcoming events and interesting information about Graceland.

We want to communicate with you and we hope you will communicate with us also. Remember, with your $20.00 annual subscription to the "Graceland Insider" you also receive a beautiful silver etching of Graceland and a card entitling you to a 10% discount on Graceland merchandise either from our mail order catalog or from our gift shop. So let us hear from you! And here's wishing all of you the very best in the New Year . . . from all of us at Graceland!

Graceland newsletter wishing all recipients a Happy Holiday, January 1983.

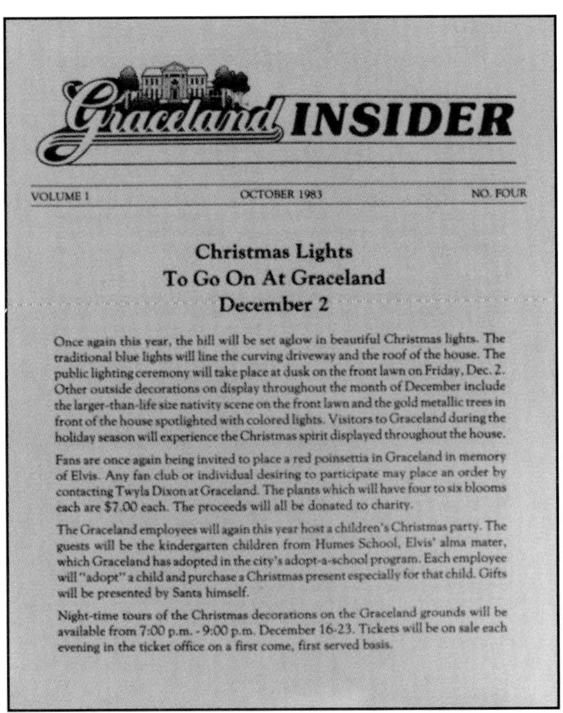

Graceland INSIDER

VOLUME 1 OCTOBER 1983 NO. FOUR

Christmas Lights
To Go On At Graceland
December 2

Once again this year, the hill will be set aglow in beautiful Christmas lights. The traditional blue lights will line the curving driveway and the roof of the house. The public lighting ceremony will take place at dusk on the front lawn on Friday, Dec. 2. Other outside decorations on display throughout the month of December include the larger-than-life size nativity scene on the front lawn and the gold metallic trees in front of the house spotlighted with colored lights. Visitors to Graceland during the holiday season will experience the Christmas spirit displayed throughout the house.

Fans are once again being invited to place a red poinsettia in Graceland in memory of Elvis. Any fan club or individual desiring to participate may place an order by contacting Twyla Dixon at Graceland. The plants which will have four to six blooms each are $7.00 each. The proceeds will all be donated to charity.

The Graceland employees will again this year host a children's Christmas party. The guests will be the kindergarten children from Humes School, Elvis' alma mater, which Graceland has adopted in the city's adopt-a-school program. Each employee will "adopt" a child and purchase a Christmas present especially for that child. Gifts will be presented by Santa himself.

Night-time tours of the Christmas decorations on the Graceland grounds will be available from 7:00 p.m. - 9:00 p.m. December 16-23. Tickets will be on sale each evening in the ticket office on a first come, first served basis.

Graceland newsletter informing recipients about the Graceland Christmas Light Ceremony, October 1983.

Graceland Christmas wishes, inside the Graceland Insider.

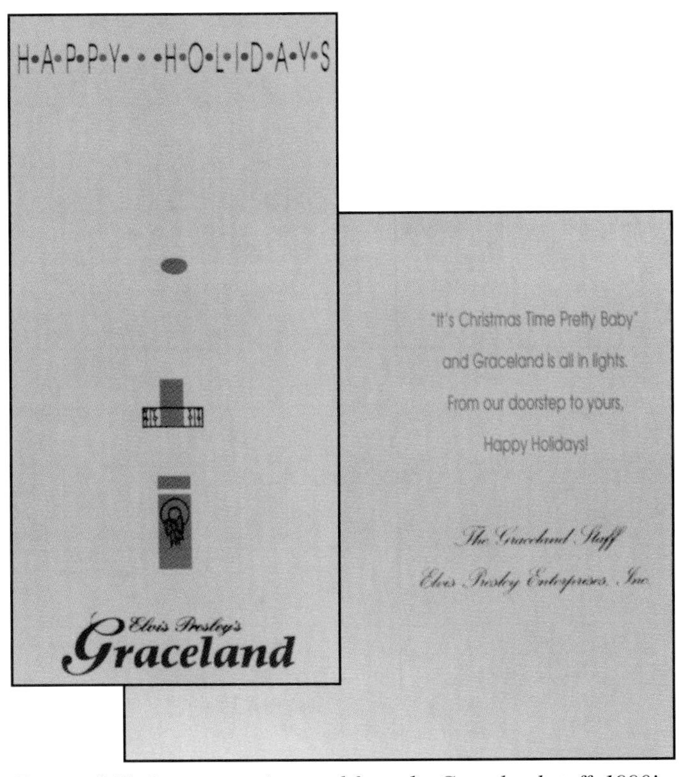

Personal Christmas greeting card from the Graceland staff, 1990's.

Keychains depicting Graceland at Christmas, sold at Graceland, 1990's.

Fan photo greeting card.

Fan photo greeting card.

Fan photo greeting card.

Christmas ornament ball from Graceland.

Christmas greeting card, sold at Graceland, 1980's.

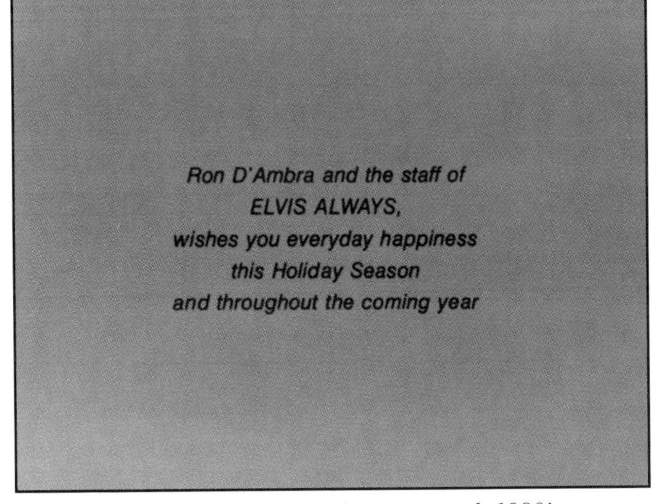

Inside the Graceland Christmas card, 1980's.

Christmas greeting card by Burnette.

Christmas greeting card, January 8, 1985, commemorates Elvis's 50th birthday.

Fan club Christmas greeting card.

Graceland Christmas ornament ball.

Christmas greeting card sold at Graceland, 1982.

Christmas greeting card sold at Graceland, 1982.

Coffee mug from Graceland, 1980's.

Christmas greeting card sold at Graceland, 1982.

Christmas postcard sold at Graceland, 1987.

Oversized (8 x 10) postcard from Graceland, 1990's.

Christmas ornament ball by Design Works, Inc.

French fan club photo greeting card.

Graceland Christmas gift catalog.

Very rare New Year's Eve party invitation sent by Elvis to guests. Held at the Manhattan Club, Memphis, December 31, 1962. Postmarked December 28, 1962.

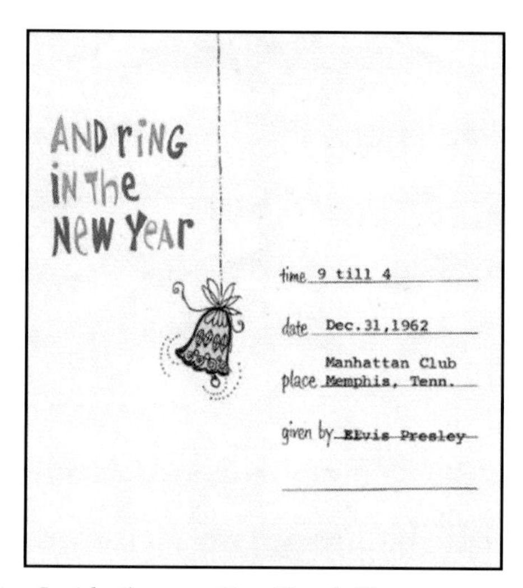

AND RING IN THE NEW YEAR

time 9 till 4

date Dec.31,1962

place Manhattan Club Memphis, Tenn.

given by Elvis Presley

Inside the rare New Year's Eve party invitation sent by Elvis.

Elvis poses in front of his Buick Riviera outside the Manhattan Club in Memphis where he held his New Year's Eve party on December 31, 1962.

Chapter 21
New Year's with Elvis

Full-page pinup of Elvis from Everybody's *magazine, Australia, January 3, 1968.*

Back cover of a fan club publication.

Back cover of a fan club publication.

Fan club photo greeting card.

Fan club photo greeting card.

Fan club Christmas postcard.

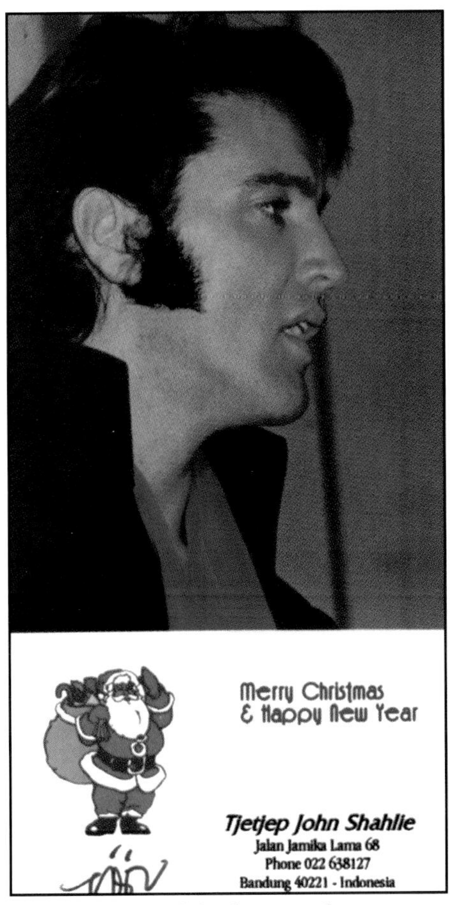

Fan club photo card.

Fan club Christmas postcard.

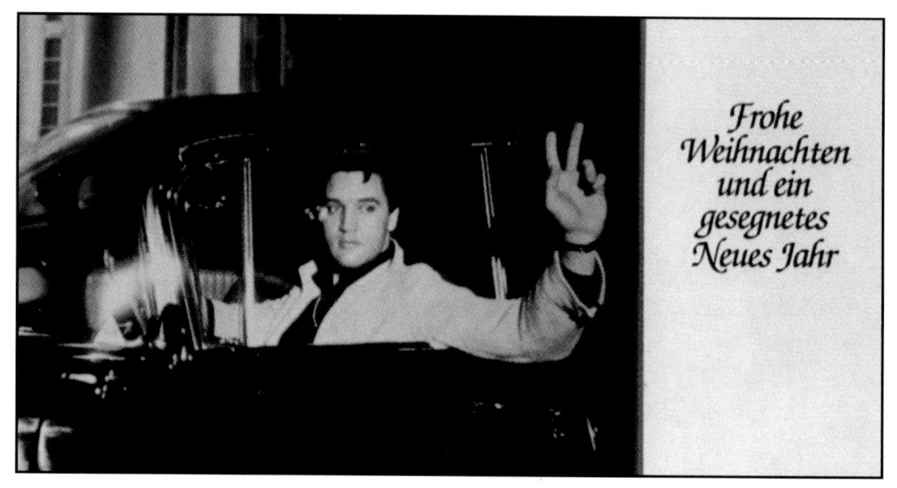

Foreign fan photo greeting card.

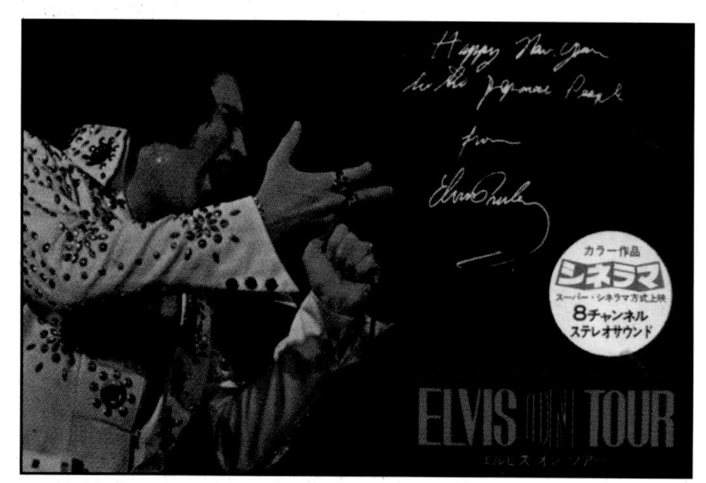

RCA Japanese postcard with a special Christmas greeting from Elvis, 1972/73.

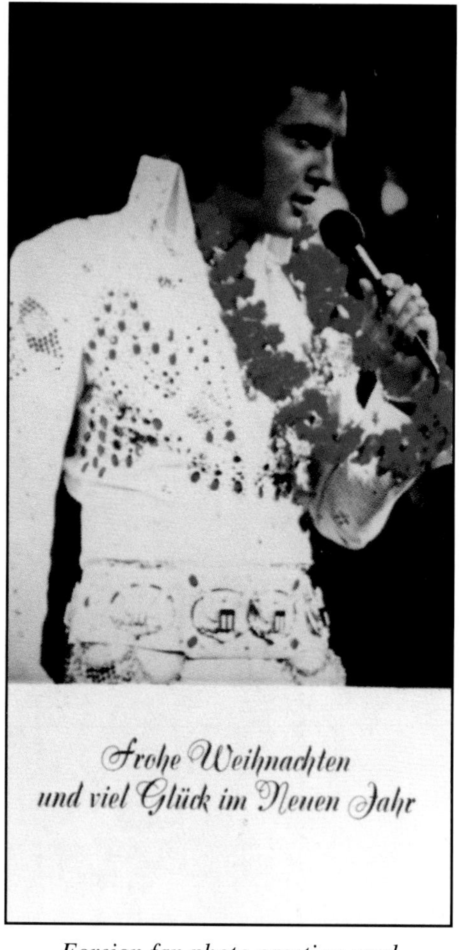

Foreign fan photo greeting card.

Fan photo greeting card.

"The Eternal Handshake." Elvis shakes the hand of author Jim Curtin in thanks for the Bicentennial Liberty Bell. New Year's Eve, December 31, 1976, Pittsburgh, Pennsylvania.

Chapter 22
An Author's Christmas

On June 28, 1976, Elvis was scheduled to appear at the Philadelphia Spectrum in my hometown of Philadelphia, Pennsylvania. As 1976 was the year of the Bicentennial, I decided to present Elvis with a gift of a Liberty Bell. The hand-crafted bell that I had custom-made for Elvis weighed 7.5 pounds and was made of solid brass. I also had a special plaque made on which the bell was to rest. The engraving on the plaquc was done by a direct descendent of George Washington.

On June 27, Elvis arrived at the Hilton Hotel on Packer Avenue. He sent word for me to come see him the following evening before the show, and when I arrived at the hotel, I was shocked. Already dressed in his prehistoric bird jumpsuit and a blue silk shirt, Elvis looked pale and sick. When I touched his arm, he was burning hot with fever. I decided that the time was not right to present Elvis with the Liberty Bell. It was getting close to show time so I wished Elvis good luck and made my way out to my green Cadillac. Just as I was exiting the parking lot, a long black limousine swerved in front of me, stopped for a second, and then quickly sped off. It was Elvis! Elvis enjoyed having me chase him and I could tell by the way the driver ran through several red lights the chase was on that evening. I could see Elvis through the back window of his limousine, pointing and laughing at me. Just before his car pulled into the underground garage at the Spectrum he gave me a "thumbs up" sign.

When Elvis came out on stage that night he was in a good mood and looked a little better. As he got his guitar from Charlie Hodge, he used its shiny surface to reflect the stage lights into my face. He was enjoying teasing me. I did not meet with Elvis again that night.

Months later, I found out that Elvis was doing a special Christmas tour which included a New Year's Eve show in Pittsburgh. It was the only show scheduled in Pennsylvania and I was not about to miss it. As I planned my trip I realized that giving him the Liberty Bell that night would be ideal. It would be a Christmas, birthday, and bicentennial gift, all wrapped up in one.

On December 31, 1976, my mother Louise and I boarded an Amtrak train bound for Pittsburgh. We arrived six hours later and caught a cab to the hotel — the same hotel that Elvis was staying in. As we warmed ourselves with hot coffee, my mother suggested that I go up to Elvis's suite and give the bell to him directly. I knew that Elvis had just arrived and was most likely preparing for that evening's show, so instead I went down to the lobby in search of Joe Esposito. I bumped into Joe as he got off the elevator. He said, "Jim, he's not seeing anybody!" I was devastated. Had I done or said something wrong? I could not imagine why Elvis did not want to see me. All of his friends, including Ed Parker, were turned away. We were simply told that Elvis was not seeing anyone and was preparing for his shows. What Ed Parker and I did not know was that Elvis had lost a lot of weight prior to this show and wanted to surprise everyone with his new look. He wanted everyone to see the new Elvis for the first time as he walked out on stage.

When Elvis walked out after the "2001: Space Odyssey," he looked amazing. He was about thirty pounds lighter and looked leaner and meaner than he had in a long time.

My mother had coerced me into bringing the Liberty Bell to the show room. We were watching the show from the eighth row and Elvis had just finished singing "Jailhouse Rock" when my mother jumped to her feet, grabbed the bell out of my lap, and began to ring it! Five loud clangs rang out. Then I took the bell from my mother's hands and rang it myself, harder and louder. Elvis stopped his show and said, "What's that cow bell ringin'? Come here with that thing." Panic set in. I knew that all 16,409 Elvis fans were staring at me, offended that I had interrupted the show. But my mother pushed me into the aisle and I finally did move. The walk to the stage seemed very long, but Elvis recognized me immediately and started to laugh. "Merry Christmas, Happy New Year, Happy Birthday, and Happy Bicentennial!" I shouted. Elvis reached down and handed me the microphone. As both of our hands held the microphone he said, "Say it again, Jim!"

Elvis had never stopped his show like that or given anyone his microphone before and my knees began to shake with fear. A super bright, white spotlight was turned to shine on both Elvis and me which only added to my nervousness. As I repeated my words, I mixed them up a bit and what came out this time was: "Merry Christmas, Happy Birthday, Happy Bicentennial, and I love you!" With a smile spread across his handsome face, Elvis said, "That's very nice of you, son!" He shook my hand for all to see.

When I handed him the bell he made a joke out of pretending that it weighed more than it did. After he gave the gift to Charlie Hodge for safekeeping, I handed him the plaque and he read the inscription: "God Bless America and Elvis Presley — from your buddy, Jim Curtin." Elvis loved it. He handed me his scarf and shook my hand again. The audience then gave me a standing ovation. I was astounded.

The Liberty Bell that I gave Elvis that night is still displayed at Graceland. It was originally placed with other awards in a glass case just below the hanging guitars (one of which is the black Gibson J-200 which I gave to Elvis in 1974). The plaque has since been separated from the bell, which now hangs on the left wall in the room after the Hall of Gold. In the same room you can find the leather suit Elvis wore in The '68 Comeback Special, his and Priscilla's wedding outfits, and Elvis's 1972 Madison Square Garden press conference suit. It is the last room in the mansion before the racquetball court. Since the 1980's, both the bell and the plaque have been featured on puzzles, games, calendars, books, and postcards.

The unauthorized album, *Rockin' with Elvis New Year's Eve Pittsburgh, PA, December 31, 1976*, features my presentation of the Liberty Bell to Elvis. On the recording you can hear the bell ringing and interrupting Elvis's show. In addition, you can also hear every word that was exchanged between Elvis and me that night, including those special last words which, for as long as I live, will be pressed between the pages of my mind...

"Merry Christmas,
Happy Birthday,
Happy Bicentennial,
and I love you."

Elvis's Christmas Poem

To Dad:

I not only live for today, but for the day after today.
I have pursued my vision and reached the mountain top.
But the peak of a mountain can be a lonely place.
I want to thank you for understanding.
I learned early in life that only by fulfilling existence
with an aim, could I find an inner peace.

I want to thank you for giving me intangible gifts.
You gave me gifts from your heart—understanding, tolerance
and concern.
You gave me gifts of your mind—purpose, ideas and projects.
You gave me gifts of your words—encouragement, empathy and solace.

Respect is avid: it wants to contain everything.
For you—my father, my friend, my confidante—
I have an avid respect.

Thanks for always being near the top of the mountain
when I needed you.

Your son,
Elvis.

This poem, written by Elvis, was given to his father, Vernon, for Christmas in 1975. Elvis had it mounted on a plaque when he gave it to Vernon. The plaque still hangs at Graceland.

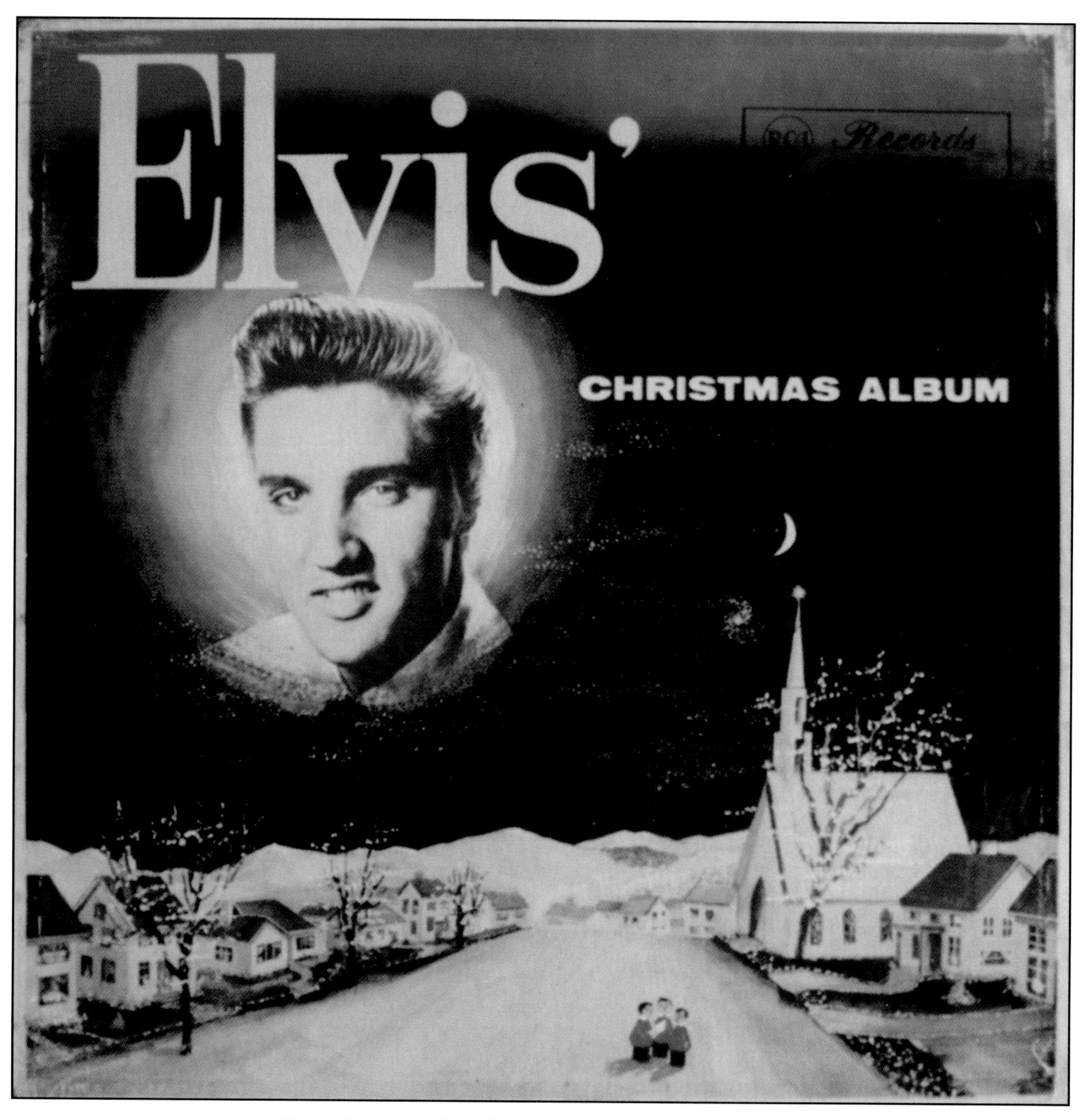

Elvis's Christmas Album *from New Zealand, 1957 (LOC-1035).*

A Christmas Discography

Christmas Songs Recorded by Elvis Presley

"Blue Christmas"
"Here Comes Santa Claus"
"Holly Leaves and Christmas Trees"
"If Everyday Was Like Christmas"
"I'll Be Home for Christmas"
"If I Get Home on Christmas Day"
"I'll Be Home on Christmas Day"
"It Won't Seem Like Christmas (Without You)"
"O Come, All Ye Faithful"
"O Little Town of Bethlehem"
"On A Snowy Christmas Night"
"Merry Christmas Baby"
"Santa Claus is Back in Town"
"Santa Bring My Baby Back to Me"
"Silent Night"
"Silver Bells"
"The First Noel"
"White Christmas"
"Winter Wonderland"
"Wonderful World of Christmas"

Elvis Presley Christmas Albums

RCA LABEL:
Elvis' Christmas Album (LOC-1035), 1957 (a ten-page color booklet enclosed)
Elvis' Christmas Album (LPM-1951), Nov. 1958 (reissue, Monoaural)
Elvis Sings the Wonderful World of Christmas (LSP-4579), Oct. 1971
Elvis Sings the Wonderful World of Christmas (ANL1-1936), Nov. 1976 (reissue, Stereo)
Elvis, Memories of Christmas (CPL1-4395), 1982 (Stereo)

RCA LABEL, VARIOUS ARTISTS:
October Christmas Sampler (SPS-3354), 1959 (promotional album, features Elvis's "Blue Christmas" from his LPM-1951 album)
Christmas Programming from RCA-Victor (SP-3366), 1960 (promotional album, has 12 complete selections from RCA-Victor Christmas albums, features Elvis's "I'll Be Home for Christmas" from his LPM-1951 album)
The Brightest Stars of Christmas (DPL1-0086), 1974 (sold only in JC Penney stores, features Elvis and ten other artists)
A Christmas Treasury of Classics from Avon (DPL1-0716), 1985 (features Elvis and nine other artists)

CAMDEN LABEL:
Elvis' Christmas Album (CAL-2428), Nov. 1970

PICKWICK LABEL:
Elvis' Christmas Album (CAS-2428), Dec. 1975 (Monaural)

CANDLELITE LABEL:
All-Time Christmas Favorites (CE-505), 1970 (five LP box set, features the following Elvis songs on one side of one album: "O Come, All Ye Faithful," "The First Noel," "If I Get Home on Christmas Day," "Silver Bells," "I'll Be Home for Christmas," and "Winter Wonderland")

TIME-LIFE ALBUMS, VIA MAIL-ORDER ONLY:
Treasury of Christmas (50 songs by various artists, TV offer, features Elvis's "Here Comes Santa Claus," 2CDs or 2 cassettes, mail to Dept. 1 - Richmond, VA 23280)
Country Christmas, 1997 (various artists, sold only on the cable channel TNT, features Elvis's "Blue Christmas" and "I'll Be Home for Christmas," 2 CDs [$29.99] or 2 Cassettes [$19.99])

Elvis Presley Christmas 45rpm Records

RCA LABEL:
"Blue Christmas" / "Blue Christmas" (HO7W-0808), 1957 (promotional record)
"Santa Claus is Back in Town" / "Blue Christmas" (447-0647), 1965
"If Everyday Was Like Christmas" / "How Would You Like to Be" (47-8950), 1966
"O Come All Ye Faithful" / "Merry Christmas Baby" (74-0572), 1971
"Blue Christmas" / "Santa Claus is Back in Town" (447-0647), 1971
"Merry Christmas Baby" / "Santa Claus is Back in Town" (PB-14237), 1977
"Blue Christmas" / "Wooden Heart" (447-0720)

Elvis Presley Christmas EP (Extended Play) Records

RCA LABEL:
Elvis Sings Christmas Songs (EPA-4108), Nov. 1957
Christmas with Elvis (EPA-4340), 1959

Elvis Presley Christmas Reel-to-Reel Tapes

The Elvis Presley Special Christmas Program (EPC-1), Dec 3, 1967 (7.5 reel-to-reel tape from the original radio broadcast, includes a word-for-word script from the program)

Elvis Presley Christmas 8-Track Tapes

Stereo-8 RCA LABEL:
Elvis Sings Songs of Christmas (P8S-1249)
Elvis Sings the Wonderful World of Christmas (P8S-1809), 1971
Elvis, Memories of Christmas (CPS1-4395), 1982

Stereo-8 RCA VARIOUS ARTISTS:
The Brightest Stars of Christmas (DPS1-0086), 1974

Stereo-8 CAMDEN LABEL:
Elvis' Christmas Album (C8S-9001), 1970

Stereo-8 PICKWICK LABEL:
Elvis' Christmas Album (C8S-9001), 1982

SUPER PLAY - TWIN PACK - PICKWICK LABEL:
contains 2 Long Play 8-track tapes, both in stereo
Elvis' Christmas Album / You'll Never Walk Alone (D82-5005)
Elvis' Double Dynamite (D82-5001), 1975

Elvis Presley Christmas Cassettes

RCA LABEL:
Elvis Sings the Wonderful World of Christmas (PK-1809), 1971
Elvis, Memories of Christmas (CPK1-4395), 1982
Elvis' Christmas Album (CAK-2428), 1985 (RCA/Camden—Special Products)
Elvis' Christmas Album (AFK1-5486), 1985
Elvis Sings the Wonderful World of Christmas (ANK1-1986), 1986 (reissue)
Elvis Presley—If Everyday Was Like Christmas (66482-4), 1994

CASSETTE SINGLE:
"Blue Christmas" / "Santa Claus is Back in Town" (0647-4-RS), 1987

Elvis Presley Christmas CDs

Elvis Presley, Merry Christmas (PCD1-5301), 1984
Elvis' Christmas (CAD1-2328), 1985 (by Special Music Co.)
Elvis, Memories of Christmas (4395-2-R), 1987
Elvis' Christmas Album (PCD1-5486), 1987
Elvis Sings the Wonderful World of Christmas (4579-2-R), 1988

Elvis Christmas Classics (9801-2-R), 1989
Elvis Presley, Blue Christmas (59800-2), 1992
Elvis Presley, If Everyday Was Like Christmas (66482-2), 1994
Elvis Presley and Jim Reeves—Christmas Favorites (ATCD-2107-2), 1991 (by Audio Treasures)
Christmas Memories from Elvis and Alabama (ATCD-2106-2), 1993 (by Audio Treasures)
Elvis—King of Rock-n-Roll—with Blue Christmas (62404-2), 1992
The Best of Christmas (7013-2-R)
Billboard Greatest Christmas Hits—1955 to the Present (R21K-70636)
We Wish You A Merry Christmas (2294-2-R)
If Everyday Was Like Christmas (07863-66482-4)
Christmas with Elvis, 1998

SPECIAL BOXED CDs:
Elvis' Christmas Album (PCD1-5486) (long box)
Elvis Presley—If Everyday Was Like Christmas (66500-2), 1994 (Special collector's edition, long box)

Elvis Presley Christmas Music Sheets and Song Books

MUSIC SHEETS:
"Santa Claus is Back in Town," 1957
"Blue Christmas," 1957
"Santa Bring My Baby Back to Me," 1957
"If Everyday Was Like Christmas," 1966
"It Won't Seem Like Christmas (Without You)," 1971
"Holly Leaves and Christmas Trees," 1971
"If I Get Home on Christmas Day," 1971
"Silver Bells," 1971

SONG BOOKS:
Elvis Sings the Wonderful World of Christmas, 1971
Elvis / Christmas, 1970's

Elvis Presley Christmas Tribute 45rpm Records

"I Wanna Spend Christmas with Elvis" / "Painted Lips and Pigtails," Little Lambsie Penn, 1956
"I Wanna Spend Christmas with Elvis" / "Once More It's Christmas," Marlene Paula, 1956
"Elvis for Christmas" / "Happy New Year," Mad Milo (Ray Tan & Combo), 1957
"I Want Elvis for Christmas" / "The Tender Age," Holly Twins, 1957
"Santa and the Satellite," Buchanan & Goodman, 1957
"Jingle Bell Imitations," Chubby Checker, 1958
"White Christmas Part I" / "White Christmas Part II," Freddie Starr, 1975
"A Christmas Letter to Daddy" / "My Christmas Came Early," J.C. Raynor & Donna Jo, 1977

"A Christmas Tribute" / "Give Someone Your Love," Bob Luman, 1977
"Blue Christmas" / Instrumental version, Johnny Farago, 1977
"Blue Christmas Without Elvis" / "How Great Thou Art," Leigh Grady, 1977
"Bluest Christmas Ever" / "Elvis God's Ready For a Song," Chris Marshon, 1977
"Elvis, Christmas Won't Be the Same Without You," Paul White, 1977
"Goodbye Bing, Elvis and Guy" / "One More Christmas," Diana Williams, 1977
"Lonely Christmas Without Elvis" / Instrumental version, Jefferson Buzz, 1977
"We'll Have a Blue Christmas Elvis" / "Please Come Home for Christmas," Jim Matthews, M.D., 1977
"Blue Christmas," Jim Fagen, 1977
"Christmas Card for Elvis" / "Christmas Without Elvis," Patsy Sexton, 1978
"Merry Christmas" / "All I Want for Christmas is My Daddy," Michele Cody, 1978
"Elvis Won't Be Here for Christmas" / "Here Comes that Hurt Again," Linda Hughes, 1979
"Merry Christmas From Lisa Marie" / "Christmas on Our Mind," Jana Simpson, 1979
"White House Christmas Party" / "Nuke Update," Fluke & Liz, 1979
"Merry Christmas Elvis" / "I'm So Lonesome I Could Cry," Paul White
"Christmas Tribute to Elvis" / "Lonesome Weekend," Ron Corey & The Destinations, 1980
"We Wish You a Teddy Christmas" / "Dance of the Teddy Boys," Nick Satan & Rockin' Devils, 1980
"Christmas is Just A Song For Us This Year," Louise Mandrell & R.C. Bannon, 1982
"Rock-n-Roll Christmas" / "New Year's Eve Party" George Thorogood & The Destroyers, 1983
"It Won't Seem Like Christmas Without Elvis," Mike Thomas, 1980's
"Christmas In Dixie," Alabama, 1990's

Elvis Presley Christmas Tribute Albums

Santa and the Satellite Part I, Buchanan & Goodman, 1973
Santa and the Satellite Part II, Buchanan & Goodman, 1973
I Wanna Spend Christmas with Elvis, Little Lambsie Penn, 1974
I Wanna Spend Christmas with Elvis, The Holly Twins, 1976
I Wanna Spend Christmas with Elvis, Marlene Paula, 1976
I Want Elvis for Christmas, The Holly Twins, 1977
Christmas to Elvis, The Jordanaires, 1978
Rock-n-Roll Christmas, George Thorogood & The Destroyers, 1983

U.S. Album Releases

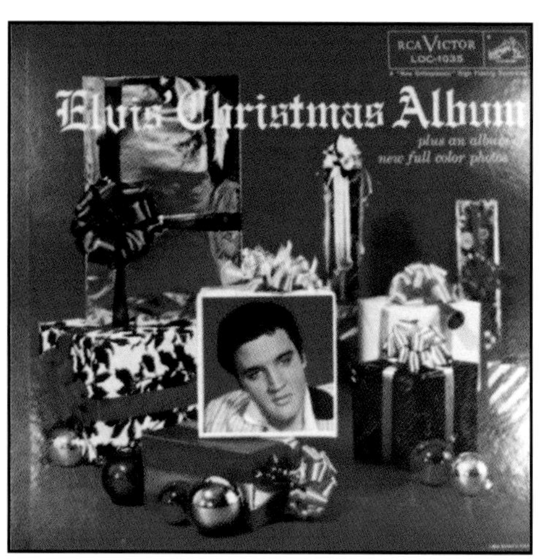

Elvis's first holiday recording, Elvis' Christmas Album *(LOC-1035, 1957).*

Photo version of the reissue of Elvis's first Christmas album, LPM-1951, released in November 1958.

Very rare promotional album released in 1960 (SP33-66). Features Elvis's "I'll Be Home for Christmas."

Elvis' Christmas Album, *re-released on the Camden label, November 1970 (CAL-2428).*

Elvis Sings the Wonderful World of Christmas *album, with bonus sticker (LSP-4579, 1971).*

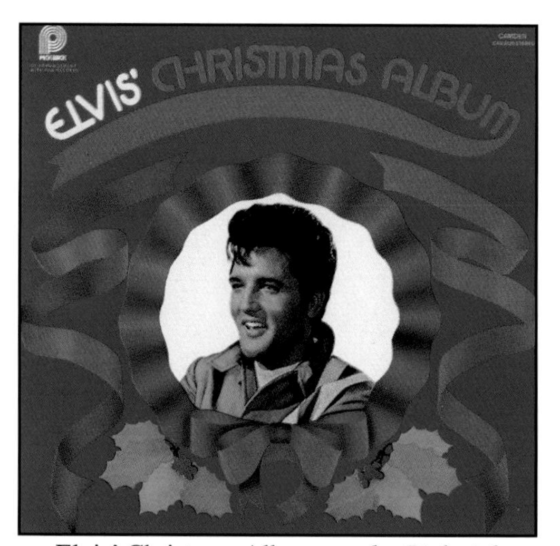

Elvis' Christmas Album *on the Pickwick label, released December 1975 (CAS-2428).*

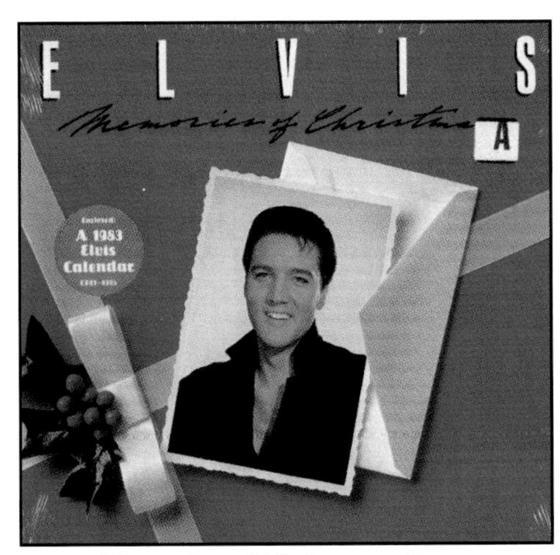

Memories of Christmas *album, released August 1982 (CPL1-4395).*

10-inch album, unauthorized edition, made in the 1980's. Contains same program as the original from 1967.

Foreign Album Releases

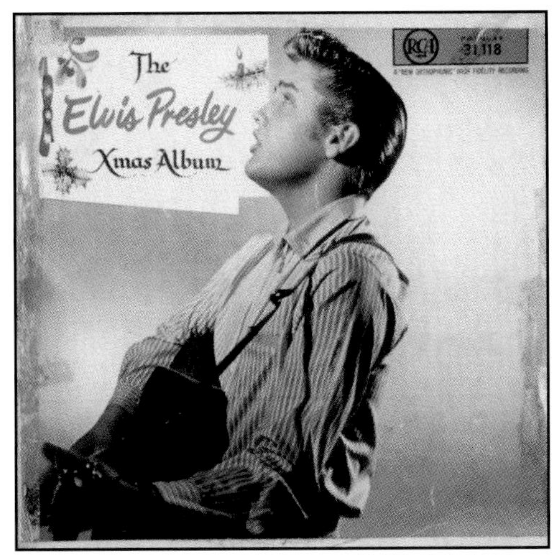

Album from South Africa, 1957 (31-118).

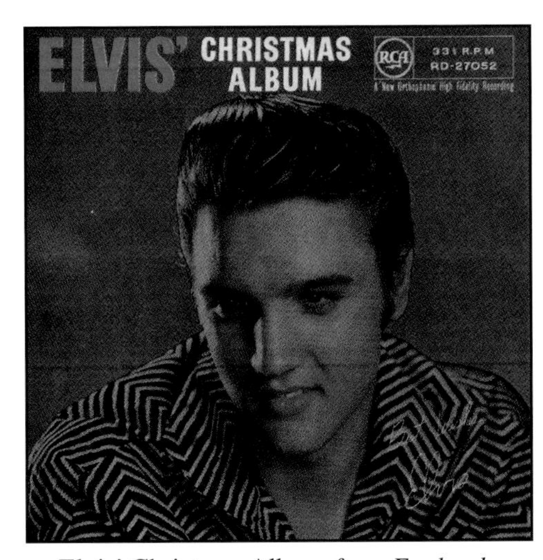

Elvis' Christmas Album *from England, November 1957 (RD-27052).*

Elvis' Christmas Album *from Germany, 1950's (LOC-1035).*

Japanese album released 1957 (LS-5038).

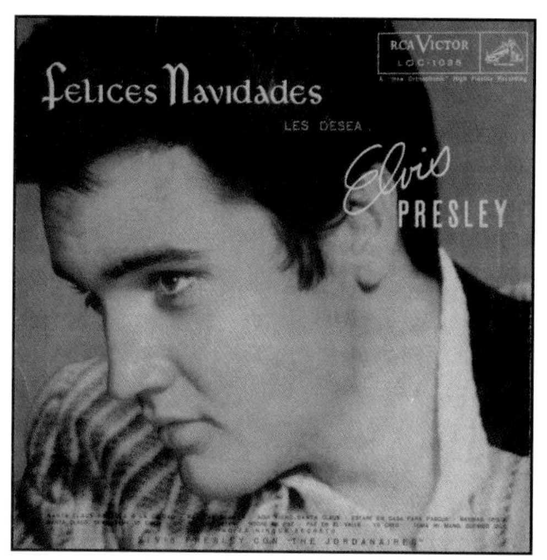

Album from Chile, 1958 (LOC-1035).

Foreign Album Releases

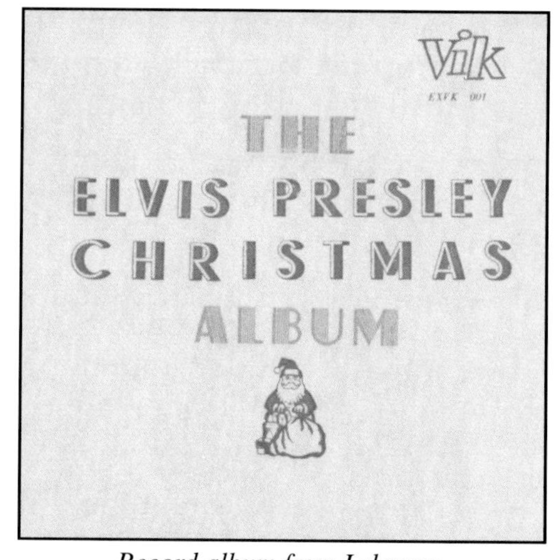

Record album from Lebanon, on the Vik label, 1959 (EXVK-001).

Elvis' Christmas Album *from Japan, 1965 (SHP-5494).*

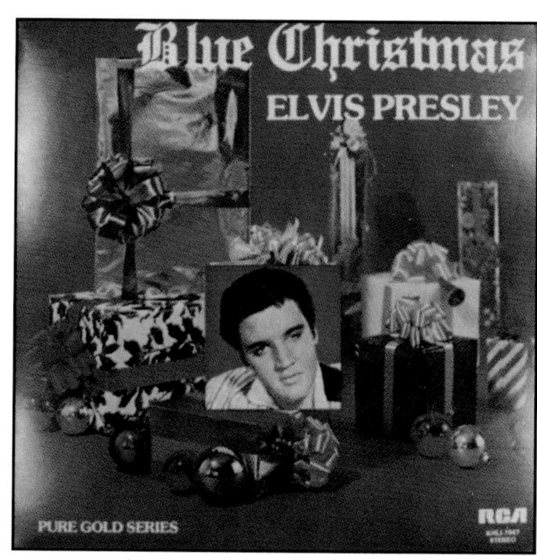

Blue Christmas *from Canada, 1976 (KNLI-7047).*

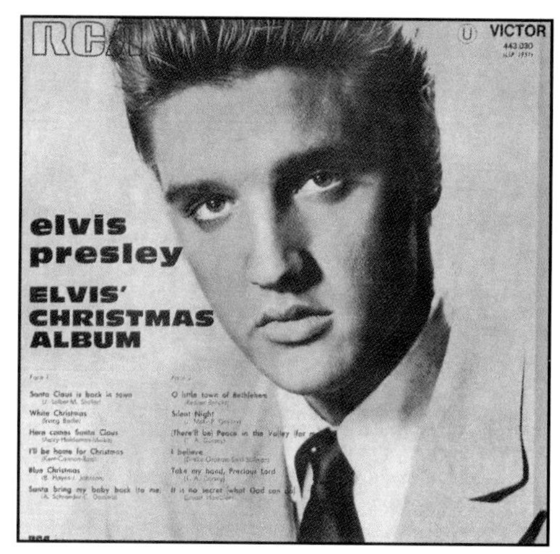

Back cover of the Elvis Sings Christmas Songs—Elvis' Christmas Album *from Paris, France, November 1971. Front cover is the same as the US release of LPM-1951.*

Elvis' Christmas Album *from England, 1970 (CDS-1155).*

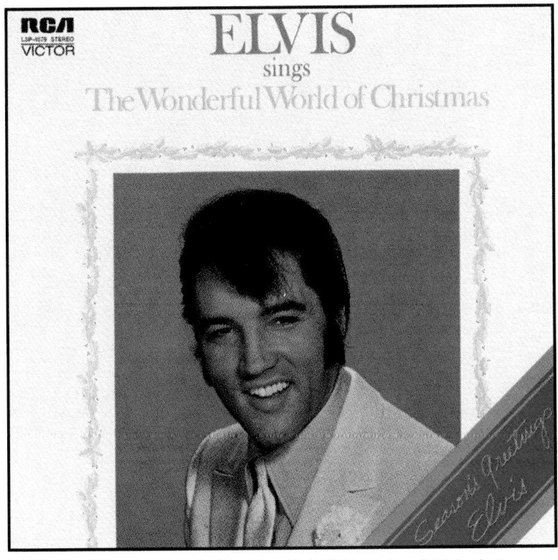

Elvis Sings the Wonderful World of Christmas *album from Germany, 1971 (LSP-4579).*

Elvis' Christmas Album *from Japan, 1972 (RCA-5028).*

A Merry Christmas from Elvis Presley *album from the Netherlands, 1982.*

12" single record, "It Won't Seem Like Christmas (Without You)" / "Merry Christmas Baby" from London, 1979.

10" single picture disc, Merry Christmas Elvis *from England, 1983 (RCAP-369). Includes "If Everyday was Like Christmas."*

U.S. 45 Singles

Original 45rpm released in November 1964.

45rpm record, RCA Gold Standard Series.
Special promotional copy, not for sale.
Recorded September 7, 1957 (447-0647).

45 rmp record picture sleeve,
released November 1966.

RCA 45rpm picture sleeve, front cover,
released December 1971.

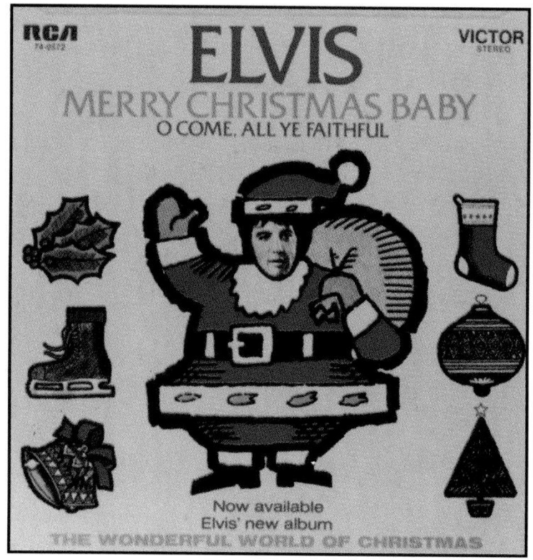

45rpm record sleeve, back cover,
released December 1971.

45rpm record, released 1977.

45rpm record sleeve,
released November 1985.

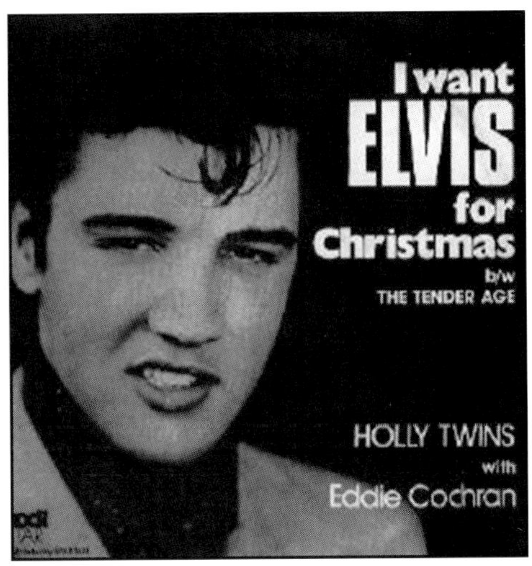

Rare 45rpm sleeve by Holly Twins
with Eddie Cochran.

Foreign
45 Singles

45rpm record from London, 1980 (PB-9627).

45rpm record from Italy,
December 1959 (45N-0939).

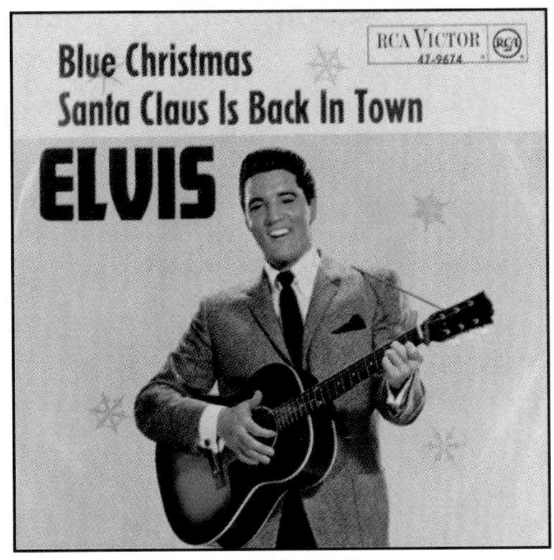

45rpm record from Germany,
1965 (47-9674).

Japanese 45 rpm record, 1950's (SS-1045).

45rpm record from Japan, October 1965 (SS-1593).

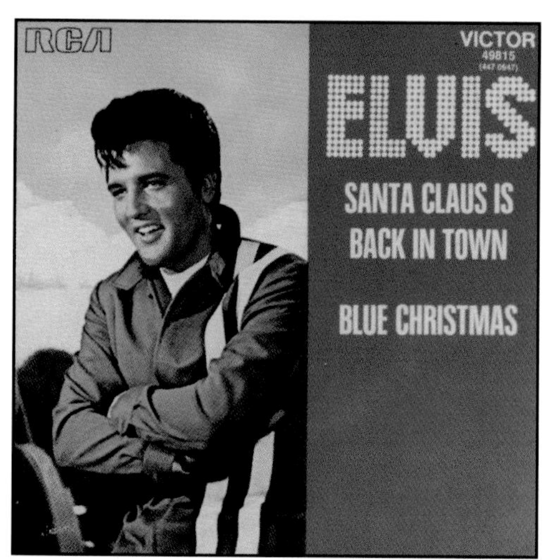

45rpm record from France, 1970's (49.815).

45rpm record from Canada, 1978 (RCA-2711).

Extended play record released November 19, 1957 (EPA-4108).

U.S. Extended Play Releases

Extended play record released November 1958 (EPA-4340).

Foreign Extended Play Releases

Extended play record from Great Britain, 1960's (RCX-121).

Back cover of the extended play record from Great Britain, 1960's (RCX-121).

Extended play record from Uruguay, 1958 (AVE-113).

Extended play record from Madrid, Spain, 1967 (3-21024).

Extended play record from Australia, 1970's (#20628).

Very rare 45rpm extended play record from Paris, France, RCA-1976 (CF-513). Comes with book containing the lyrics of the four songs on the record.

U.S. 8-tracks

Pickwick stereo 8-track tape, 1975 (C8S-9001).

RCA stereo 8-track tape (P8S1249).

RCA twin pack stereo 8-track tape, December 1975 (C8S-5051).

Pickwick stereo 8-track tape, 1975 (C8S-9001).

RCA stereo 8-track tape, 1971 (P8S-1809).

RCA stereo 8-track tape, 1982 (CPS1-4395).

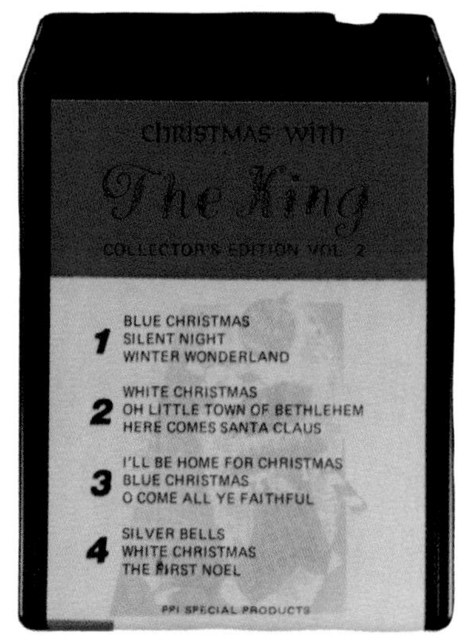

Unauthorized 8-track tape, collector's edition, Vol. 2. Christmas With the King, *by PPI Special Products, 1977.*

U.S. Cassettes

RCA cassette in long pack box, 1974 (DPS1-0086).

RCA cassette, soft box, 1971 (ANK1-1936).

RCA cassette, 1982 (CPK1-4395).

Pickwick cassette, 1985.

RCA cassette, 1985.

RCA cassette, 1992.

RCA cassette, 1992.

RCA cassette, 1994.

RCA cassette single, 1987.

Cassette, 1978.

RCA Camden cassette from England (CAM 462).

Christmas card with CD, 1995 (SLA-1). Snowmen's League of America proudly presents: 'Elvis Presley—Santa Claus is Back in Town.' *8 Elvis songs with mail envelope.*

Special promotional CD with card and envelope, by the "Snowmen's League of America," 1995.

U.S. Compact Discs

RCA Compact Disc in long pack box, 1980's.

RCA Compact Disc (PCD1-5486), 1980's.

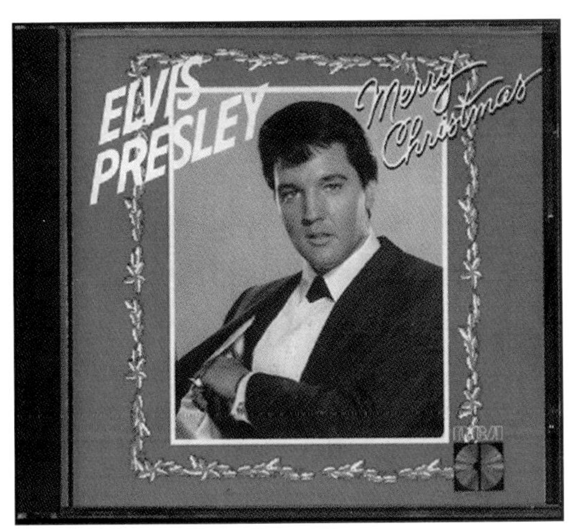

Very rare RCA Compact Disc, 1984 (PCD1-5301).

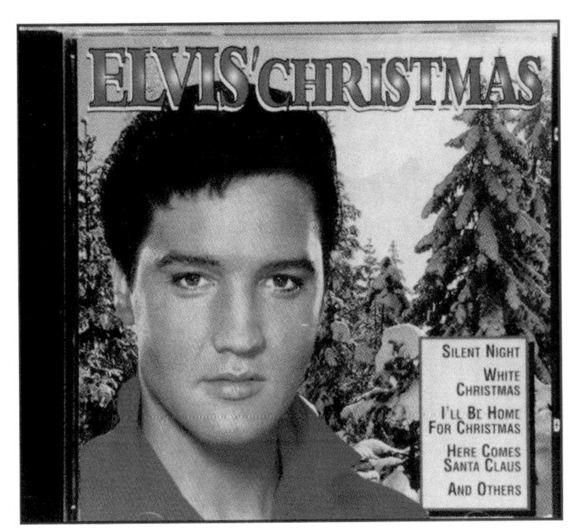

RCA Compact Disc, Special Music Company, 1985 (CAD1-2428). Features 10 Elvis songs.

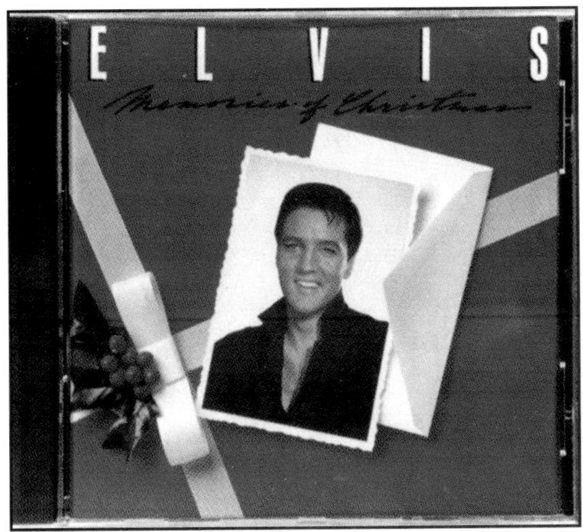

RCA Compact Disc, 1987.

RCA/BMG Compact Disc, 1988.

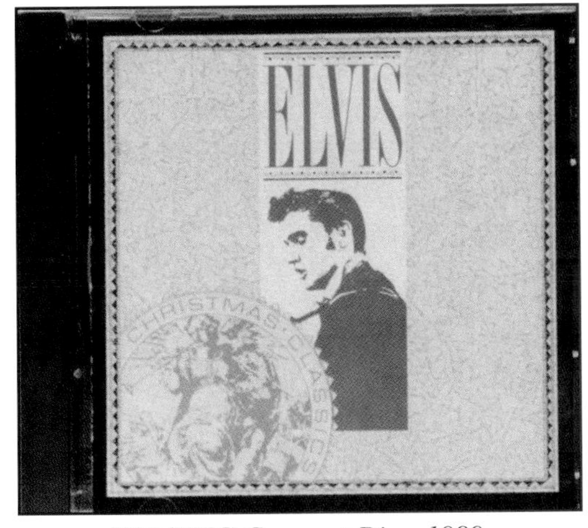

RCA/BMG Compact Disc, 1989.

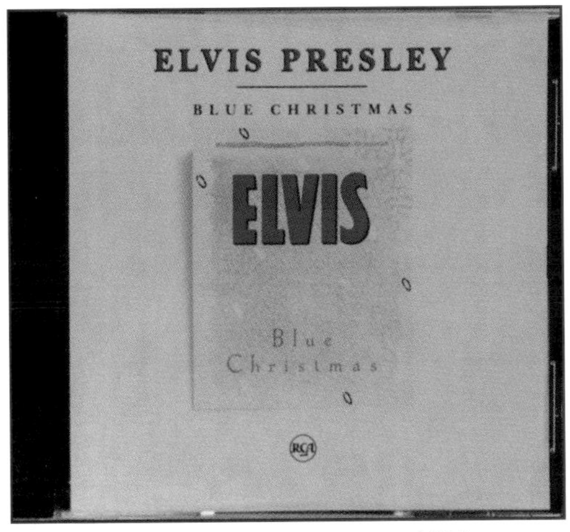

RCA/BMG Compact Disc, 1992.

RCA/BMG Compact Disc by Audio Treasures, 1993. Elvis and Jim Reeves.

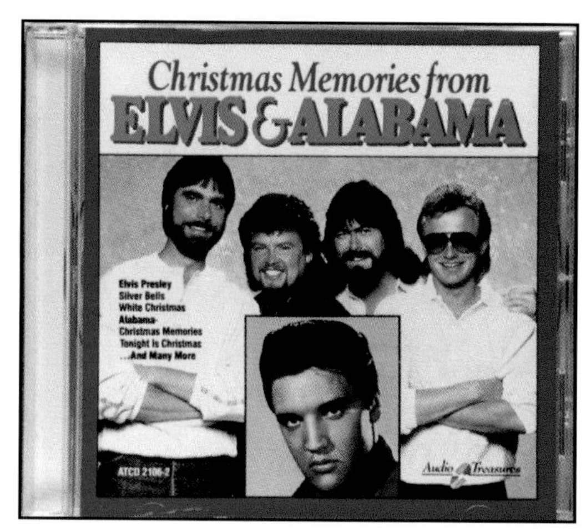

RCA/BMG Compact Disc by Audio Treasures, 1993. Elvis and Alabama.

U.S. Compact Disc Singles

RCA/BMG Compact Disc single, 1991 (PD-49149). US release features "Merry Christmas Baby" and "Silent Night."

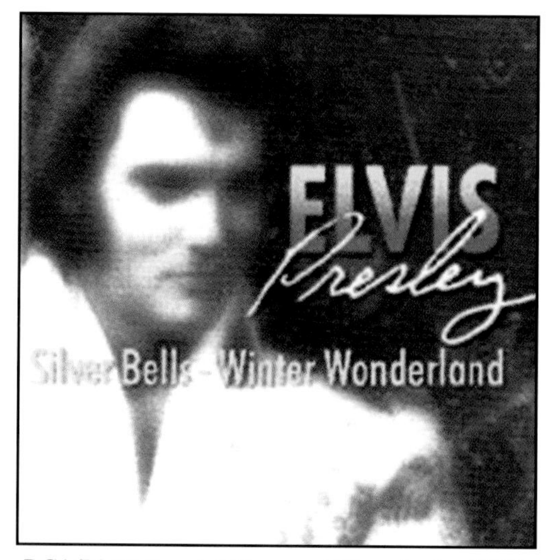

RCA/BMG Special Compact Disc single, 1998.

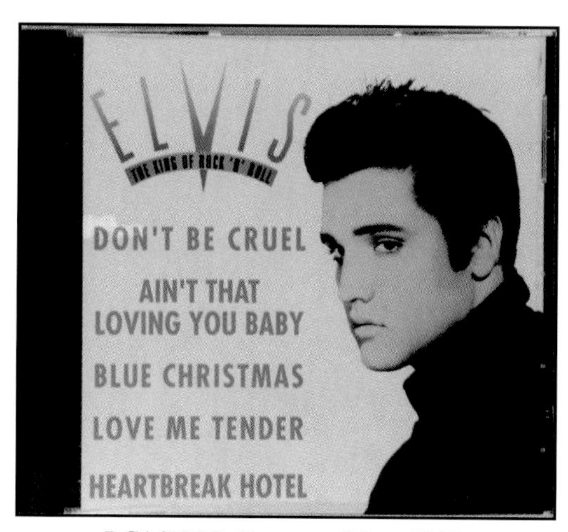

RCA/BMG Compact Disc, 1992.

World Star Collection
Foreign Compact Disc, 1987 (WSC99101).

Foreign Compact Discs

RCA/BMG Compact Disc from Germany, 1987 (ND89474).

RCA/BMG Japanese Compact Disc, 1989 (B19D41087).

RCA/BMG Japanese Compact Disc, 1990 (BVCP5031).

Club-Records Compact Disc, Germany (CR10-029 PD).

Back Biter Compact Disc from Germany, 1994 (BB61037).

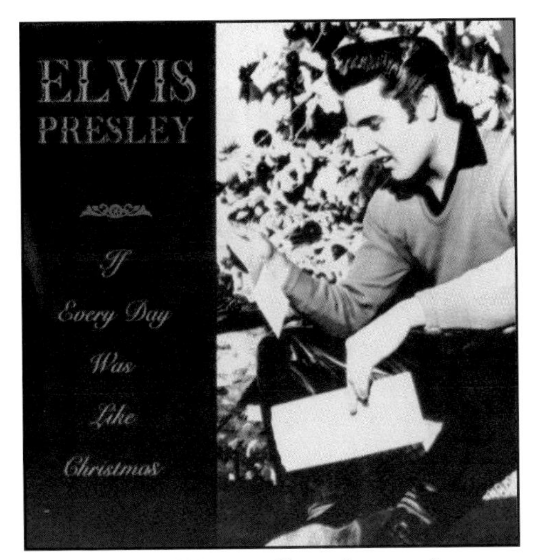

Compact Disc cardboard cover from If Everyday Was Like Christmas *box, pop-up card set, 1994.*

Inside contents of the boxed Compact Disc special collector's edition, If Everyday Was Like Christmas, *1994.*

Boxed Compact Disc, special collector's edition, RCA 1994 (66506-2-07863). Includes box, CD, and pop-up card of the Graceland mansion.

Super rare Compact Disc set given only to Elvis Presley fan club presidents for Christmas 1997. Only 500 were made. Includes Compact Disc, pictures, and autographs from Priscilla and Lisa Marie.

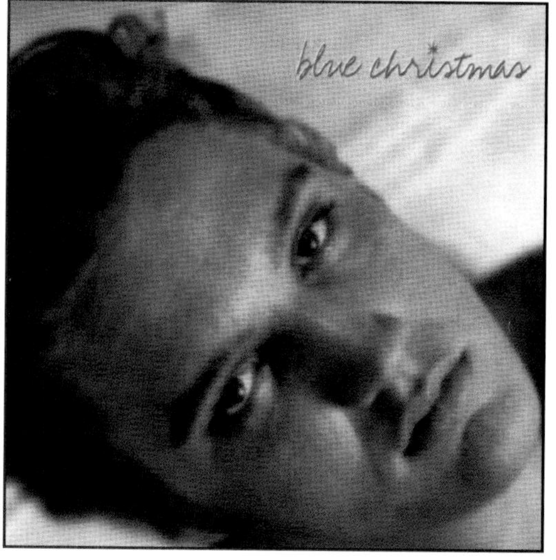

Insert picture from the special Compact Disc given to EPFC presidents, 1997.

Actual Compact Disc, Blue Christmas, *1997.*

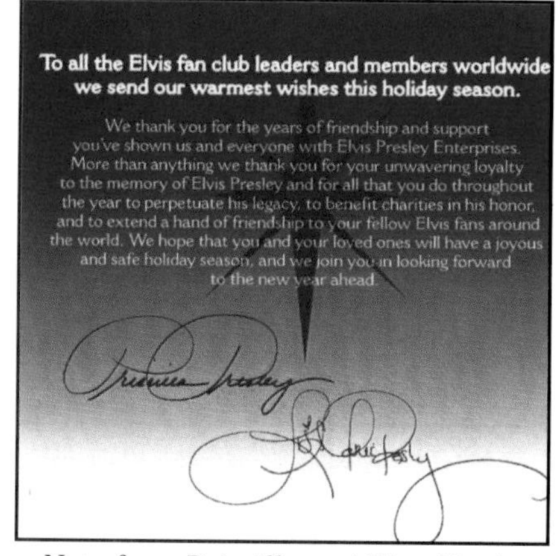

To all the Elvis fan club leaders and members worldwide we send our warmest wishes this holiday season.

We thank you for the years of friendship and support you've shown us and everyone with Elvis Presley Enterprises. More than anything we thank you for your unwavering loyalty to the memory of Elvis Presley and for all that you do throughout the year to perpetuate his legacy, to benefit charities in his honor, and to extend a hand of friendship to your fellow Elvis fans around the world. We hope that you and your loved ones will have a joyous and safe holiday season, and we join you in looking forward to the new year ahead.

Note from Priscilla and Lisa Marie, with autographs, 1997.

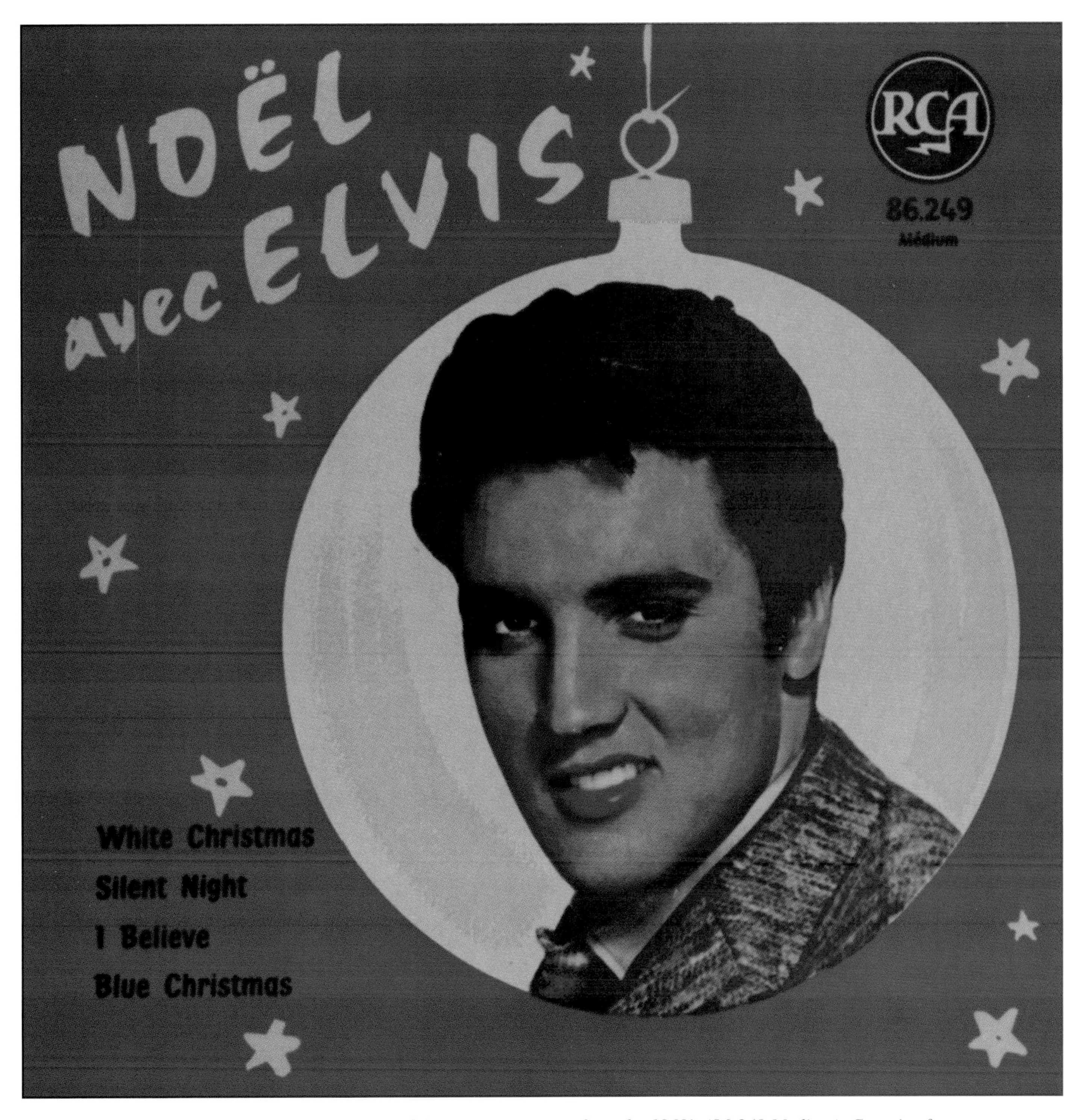

Very rare RCA 45rpm extended play record from Paris, France, from the 1960's (86-249 Medium). Contains four songs.

Acknowledgments

My sincerest thanks to Sandra Laughlin, my publisher and friend, who is also a big Elvis fan. She shares my vision and my dream of bringing out great books on Elvis. Thank you, Mrs. Laughlin, for your hard work, your patience, and your friendship!

My special thanks to Renata Ginter, for her writing and for her keen eye with the photography. You did a great job transforming all my notes and memories into this great text and in photographing my Elvis collection. It took a lot of hard work and many hours, but we did it!

Also thanks to John Laughlin and his great artwork... and Bethany Snyder for her great eye!

Personal thanks to:
Arnie Ganem—Thanks for all your help, trust and friendship.
Hee Jean and Chong Ahn (Photo Express, Upper Darby, PA)—Thank you for your great photo developing.
Joe Santella and Jim Charlier (Mail Boxes Etc., Springfield, PA)—Thanks for taking such good care of me.

Special acknowledgments to:
Elvis Presley Enterprises; the Graceland Estate; RCA-Victor; Pickwick Records; Gladys Music Inc.; Choice Music Inc.; Hill & Range Songs Inc.; Elvis Presley Music Inc.; Atlantic Music Corp.; The Aberbach Group; The Big Three Music Corp.; Anglo-Pic Music Co. Ltd.; Polygram Music Publishing; Hal Leonard Corp.; Decca Records; Russell Stover; NBC-TV; *The Ed Sullivan Show*; The River Group; *Modern People* magazine; *Ideal* magazines; Hillman Publications; *Cosmopolitan* magazine; *Photoplay* magazine; *Saturday Evening Post*; *Country Music Magazine*; *Star* magazine; *Everybody's Magazine* (Australia); *Billboard* magazine; *TV Guide*; US Post Office; Carlton Cards; Hallmark; American Greetings; Cedco Publishing; McCormick; Bradford Exchange; Delphi Plate Co.; Avon; JC Penney; Topperscot Inc.; David Schultz; Factors Inc.; Boxcar Enterprises Inc.; Las Vegas Hilton Hotel; Paramount Studios; Twentieth Century Fox Studios; United Artists Studios; Janelle McComb for her "Priceless Gift" poem; Paul Dowling (for loaning me pics to six records); American Postcard Company; Southern Postcard Company; DCI Studio; Burnette; Design Works, Inc.; Don Lancaster Photography.

A special thank you to all the Elvis fan clubs worldwide, included in this book. You have kept Elvis alive throughout this holiday with your wonderful Christmas newsletters, booklets, and greeting cards.

Photo credits: The Graceland Estate; United Press Telephoto; Associated Press; UPI Telephoto; Sean Shaver; Jimmy Velvet; Judy Palmer; Sonny West; Sue McCasland; John Herman; P. Brousseau; Virginia Coons; Sandi Miller; George Hill; The Grand Ole Opry; Bill Williams; Jim Morris (King's Court Fan Club). Front cover photo: Paramount Studios.
If we have left out anyone ... it was not on purpose!

Elvis drinks a glass of orange juice on Christmas morning, 1976. This was Elvis's last Christmas.